Mike Ganley, along with his wife Jojanneke (Jo), run a guesthouse in Harrogate, North Yorkshire. Mike gave up full-time teaching in 2008 and with a PhD in Cultural Anthropology. He believes he's the highest qualified chambermaid in Yorkshire. He has a daughter in Seville and a son in Berlin.

To Jojanneke – my partner in life, love, and scrambled eggs on toast.

Mike Ganley

ROOMS TONIGHT!

AUSTIN MACAULEY PUBLISHERS™

LONDON • CAMBRIDGE • NEW YORK • SHARJAH

A CIP catalogue record for this title is available from the British Library.

ISBN 9781788788656 (Paperback)
ISBN 9781528956284 (Epub e-book)

www.austinmacauley.com

First Published (2019)
Austin Macauley Publishers Ltd
25 Canada Square
Canary Wharf
London
E14 5LQ

Thanks to my mate, Bigsy, for encouraging me at the very start of the project and badgering me for updates during our drinking sessions in Leeds. Also, a big thank you to my late uncle, Alex Ganley, who only got to proofread the early chapters: I miss his laughter on the other end of the telephone. Lastly, thanks to Juan Luis Carmona Moreno for coming up with the cover idea.

Introduction

Ten years ago, I decided I'd had enough of teaching. After being in the profession for about 30 years, I thought I'd try my hand at something else. I suppose it was my mid-life crisis. I had wasted hours drooling over an MG MGB Roadster on the internet. British racing green with a full reconditioned engine – and of course, my initials were MG so I was trying to persuade myself it was the obvious decision to make.

Jo, my wife, was unimpressed. She thought a man of my age and physique would struggle squeezing into a sports car and so it was left to Plan B. Instead of a sports car, it was a guest house! The initial plan was to buy a cosy cottage in the Yorkshire Dales – the sort with beamed ceilings, inglenook fireplaces and obviously a dog in front of the range fire – but then, reality kicked in. For a start, my wife Jo, is allergic to dogs! Then there was the problem of how does one make a living in the winter months when tourism grinds to a halt? Perhaps the Dales would be fine for someone wanting to top up on their pension during the summer months, but as a sound business venture, we needed to look elsewhere.

Yes, we British have an obsession for guest houses or B&Bs. Any afternoon TV schedule is incomplete without several episodes of *Four in a Bed*. When we go away for a short break or weekend, staying in a B&B or guest house is something quintessentially British. Driving round, looking for a "Vacancies Tonight" sign displayed in a window used to be (and perhaps still is for some) a key feature of a short break or holiday. Not only do guest houses or B&Bs provide the traveller with the basic necessities of a warm room, a bed for the night, washing/showering facilities and a cooked breakfast the next day, they also offer the unique possibility of engaging the proprietor in conversation, finding more about the area or town they are visiting and meeting a friendly face in an unfamiliar part of the country.

Guest houses are rarely anonymous. Anyone suffering with acute shyness would be advised to book into a hotel where they will be treated with more anonymity. Conversations, with proprietors or fellow guests (usually at breakfast), are almost inevitable. You will be quizzed on where you come from and what you do there. You will be given tips on where, and more importantly, where not to go and you will instantly have a feel for the area you are visiting. Guests from overseas will be totally immersed in British culture; stay in a family run B&B and really experience the British way of life is the advice given by VisitBritain, the organisation awarding the star rating system for B&Bs and guest houses.

It might be useful at this point to outline the basic difference between a B&B and a guest house. Technically, a B&B is a private house offering accommodation for no more than six paying guests. A guest house is run on a more commercial basis and provides accommodation for more than six guests, though normally does not offer the facilities and amenities a hotel would have such as guest lounge, bar or restaurant.

In the early days, visitors would stumble on a B&B or guest house by accident, walking or driving around. Nowadays, many people are able to book in advance as owners advertise in local visitor and holiday guides. Both the AA and VisitBritain produce guides to holiday accommodation and these are also the two bodies who, between them, award the star rating system the B&Bs and guest houses proudly display in their windows and promotional literature. More recently, the internet has added another dimension to choosing and booking accommodation. Websites are designed to entice guests with information and photographs, and at the click of a button, customers are able to see what rooms are available, at what price and book the room from the comfort of their own home.

Years ago, guests often had to share bathrooms, and I'm sure many of us recall hopping outside the bedroom only to find an engaged sign on the bathroom or toilet. Today, the majority of rooms are fully "en-suite" and though B&Bs traditionally didn't offer the same level of comfort and quality as a hotel, the difference is narrowing.

It's hard to label people who stay in guest houses as opposed to hotels. We have entertained people from all walks of life, political persuasions, occupations and accents. I'd like to think they are more individual spirits than folk who simply book into a hotel. They are probably more adventurous, enjoy meeting people and want to get out and about rather than sitting in a guest lounge for most of the day. They probably will want to sample different restaurants, drink in different locals and make the most of their time in any one area. The bottom line is they will be more actively involved in discovering an area rather than being there simply to relax.

Running a B&B or guest house requires no qualifications or experience. Some people start by simply putting a "Vacancies" or "Rooms Tonight" sign in their window. Anyone looking for somewhere to stay for the night would see the sign and knock at your door. That's the theory anyway. It is an easy way of making a few bob on the side. The recent rise in the Airbnb market is a testament to this. According to *The Times*, running a bed-and-breakfast is one of the most straightforward small business model, and can "provide a rewarding and flexible lifestyle for naturally hospitable people". Certainly the majority of people my wife and I met staying in various guest houses up and down the country would confirm this (although there was one notable exception!), and our experiences staying in such places undoubtedly sowed the seeds for our own plans to run one.

Running a guest house is the ideal semi-retirement plan: escaping the rat race, buying a property in a favourite tourist area and sitting back watching the money come rolling in for much less work than before (in my case teaching) is the dream.

Or at least that is what I thought it was.

To start with, the "sit back" bit is far removed from reality. In fact, during the first three months of running our guest house, I lost nearly a stone with all the running up and down the stairs I did. Admittedly, much of this running up and down was unnecessary. Often I'd get to the top room (four flights of stairs) only to realise I'd left the new toilet roll downstairs and therefore had to go all the way back down again. Imagine this scenario repeated on a regular daily basis. Then there's all the bending over to make beds – does wonders for the waistline!

And as far as the watching the money come rolling in bit is concerned – well, it does, but the problem is, it rolls out even quicker.

And if I thought I was escaping anywhere, the endless telephone calls from insurance brokers, advertisement companies and website designers as well as waiting hours for guests who had forgotten to tell you what time they were due to arrive, reminded me that this was in no way, shape or form, an escape!

Since moving here, we have spoken to numerous people who told me it was also their dream to run a guest house. If so, I apologise in advance for putting them off the idea!

Similarly, if people are reading this because they are fascinated with the idea of a lifestyle change and the current obsession with giving up the "rat race", then once again, this book is not intended to be a guide or lifestyle manual.

There are many good handbooks giving advice and tips for both; would be guest house proprietors, as well as, any fulfilling other potential lifestyle change from sailing around the world to learning to paint.

The book wasn't written for any of these reasons. Neither is the book a literary ego trip. I tried editing myself out, but it somehow didn't work. You see, everything was seen through my eyes and that's why you are stuck with me, but I am not the purpose or rationale behind the book.

If anyone had suggested that I should write about my change of occupation, life style or the day-to-day experiences as a guest house proprietor, I would have laughed at them: this would be indulgence at its most base level.

This book simply grew out of the numerous hilarious, amusing, shocking and at times, heart-warming experiences we had running the guesthouse: every time something "happened", there was a nagging inner voice telling me to record it. Why, I don't know. I suppose, in years to come, we might enjoy looking back and remembering the experiences we had, but the first rumblings of a book came from friends who, every time we met, would always pester us for the latest amusing happenings.

Seeing them roll around in fits of laughter started the "ball rolling" and several of the stories – for example, the gentleman we thought was an author finally convinced me; although I have a reasonably lively imagination, even I could not have imagined some of the incredulous "things" that happened.

From that moment on, the idea of a book was hatched.

Everything you will read in this short collection of stories, happenings, events – call them what you like – are completely true. They happened over a ten year period, starting with the transition to such a massive lifestyle change, and recall the exploits and antics of the more colourful and memorable guests staying with us since.

Spare moments, waiting for guests to come down to breakfast or resting between changing rooms (that happens a lot now!), were the times when I'd jot down something, recall a funny – or maybe a not so funny – event, or simply try to describe a very unusual situation with vocabulary clearly insufficient for the task.

Even now, the amusing incidents continue to happen. As I am sitting here in front of my laptop, I have just heard a scream from the dining room. It is early on a Sunday morning, and at least there was only one customer there!

I ran immediately to find out what had happened. The poor chap took a first sip of his tea and realised that the sugar bowl was full of salt!

'Is somebody here trying to poison me?' he yelled as I mumbled apologetically, scraping away the fine white substance at the top of the sugar bowl to reveal the granulated sweet stuff underneath.

I replaced it and mumbled an apology of sorts before checking the remainder of the sugar bowls: they all had to be replaced!

The obvious parallels have been drawn with *Fawlty Towers*. Whilst we haven't had a rat (or was it a Siberian hamster?) running about the place, we have had delightful German guests who return regularly. We have had psychologists who have talked to us about the unique insight. Running a guesthouse gives on the human condition and we have had very, very challenging American guests – minus the Waldorf salad. As yet, we haven't had a corpse to deal with (though I know of another guest house that did!) and the Hotel Inspector did provide a few anxious moments.

Several years on, I can honestly say that the enthusiasm and excitement of running the place hasn't worn off and, more importantly, the amusing incidents continue to crop up regularly confirming that fact is really much stranger than fiction.

Mike Ganley
Harrogate
North Yorkshire

Chapter 1
Who in Their Right Mind Would
Run a Guest House?

June 2016

'Who the hell is having a shower now?' I mumbled, trying to focus on the blurred red digits on the alarm clock. It was 3:30 and water was gushing into the drain directly below the bedroom we were trying to sleep in. I listened intently. Any moment now, the sound would abate and peace would be restored, giving me another three to three and a half hours of sleep before venturing up to prepare breakfast for the thirteen paying guests.

Saturday nights were always full. Perhaps we should charge more than we do? I'd turned down three couples yesterday desperate for a somewhere to stay. Some of the more posh places were charging over £200 a night for a double room. I suppose they can charge whatever they want and rarely see guests as real people in real situations but just as statistics or price tags. I would struggle to look directly into a customer's eyes and ask for such an eye-watering sum. Those places are totally anonymous and often charge extra for breakfast as well. Then there's the Wi-Fi and the parking…

'Are you awake?'

Jo, my wife, prodded me. 'Room 2 has just got in; could hear him fumbling with the key in the lock and clambering up the stairs. I think he's having a shower now.'

I mumbled something to indicate that I was awake but not sufficiently cognisant for a full and lucid conversation. I was aware, however, that water continued to gush from the downpipe into the drain. If he was having a shower, then it was a hell of a long one. Surely no one takes that long in a shower especially at (I had another peep at the alarm clock) quarter to four in the morning! The guest was returning from a public school reunion. Large, posh bloke from London. Dr someone or other. A ringer for Boris Johnson if ever there was one.

This time the red digits were less blurred and the ensuing breakfast was being logistically prepared in my semi-comatose state. I listened to the water continue to gurgle its way down the drain though I'd only got as far as switching the water heater and plate cleaner on before sleep once again beckoned. I remember thinking that perhaps it wasn't the shower but it was raining. Of course! Rain had been predicted. That was it! I snuggled under the duvet and let the reassuring sounds of the rainstorm seduce me back into slumberland.

At 7:15 precisely, the alarm bleeped, and it was only when I turned off the annoying repetitive noise that I noticed the rain had not slackened one bit. It seemed as resolute as ever – determined to replenish all three reservoirs along the Erewash valley. Thoughts ran across my mind of the pending drought several years ago when chimney stacks of long since flooded villages were once again rising above the impoverished reservoir surfaces. With this altruistic attitude, I dressed and ran upstairs to start the breakfast preparations and, of course, to put on the kettle to make Jo a cup of tea (she was definitely not a morning person) – though she would happily stay up late to await guests when I was nodding asleep in front the evenings' second visit to Coronation Street.

The first thing I noticed was the bright sunshine and how dry the courtyard was. Strange! It had not rained at all! I ventured outside into the bright morning sunshine and, as well as hearing the bird chirping and the odd car passing by, could also hear the unmistakable sound of water rushing down into the drain. Now I know the sound of running water is considered to be therapeutic, and I even know a few people who have paid good money to buy soothing, relaxing CDs to help create the feeling of tranquillity but the sound of this water running into the drain was somehow not having the same effect on me.

What the hell was going on? At this point I also became aware of the heating system – working overtime to heat the very same water thundering into the drain. Surely this had not been going on all night? It didn't take a super sleuth to work out that the source of the water was Room 2 – the very same room our ex public school chap was staying in. The one who eventually got home at 3:30.

I think it was at this point when my emotions switched to a mixture of fear and anger over what all this water could possibly do. Unfortunately, it didn't take me long to work out the answer to that question. As soon as I returned inside, a few tell-tale drips told me everything I needed to know. Water was dripping from the ceiling onto the bookshelf below and I knew that if the shower or tap had not been turned off, then sooner rather than later I could expect a bucket load of further problems – literally!

A quick glance at the registrations diary showed me that Dr Ed Johns was residing in that room. I knocked on the door, quietly at first, in the hope that a few subtle raps would wake him without subjecting the whole guest house to an early (and possibly cold!) shower and breakfast. I put my ear to the door and could hear all sorts of spluttering and snorting, though I couldn't quite work out if the sounds were coming from our Boris Johnson impersonator or the shower. I tried to rap a little louder, though it was obvious that this man was out for the count. Whatever the source of the water leakage, it was here for a few hours longer and short of breaking the door down, the majority of guests would have a refreshing welcome to the Sunday morning awaiting them. I had read somewhere that a cold shower was one of the best remedies for a hangover – though I doubt whether or not guests would be so sympathetic or quick to agree.

Jo emerged wondering what the hell was going on. Before I had finished pointing up to the water dripping from the ceiling, she was storming upstairs and banging on the door of Room 2. I pointed out to her I had already done that and suggested we should just hope that the damage was kept to a minimum; I suggested we concentrate on the other 12 people who would be coming downstairs after their cold showers for a (hopefully) warm breakfast.

We soon were into the full swing of breakfasts, and as usual on a Sunday morning, the good old fashioned fry up was the main order of the day. At first, I had done all the cooking and Jo the front of house stuff, but as her confidence in the kitchen increased, she was more than happy for me to interface with a group of complete strangers in the morning while she was left alone with the range, fresh ingredients and her thoughts.

17

One or two couples seemed to take great pride informing me, in front of everyone else, that there had been no hot water that morning. I could only apologise and inform them of the unusual reason for their cold showers. You could tell who would be the complainers – although, under similar circumstances I think I would have complained as well. Some of the nicer, quieter people just nodded and smiled; you know that it would take more than a cold shower to get them to take pen to paper and write to "Watchdog". Others however, were far more, let's just say "aware" of their rights and are no doubt armed with notebooks and tablets which, at the flick of a switch (or rather the tap of an icon) would link immediately to Trip Advisor.

When we decided to run a guesthouse, Trip Advisor wasn't really that well known, and I think for about three or even four years we had just one review on it! Needless to say, things have changed considerably since then and now, only four or five years further down the road, such consumer driven web sites proliferate and we have to accept that. Most of our reviews had been excellent and the rest very good, but then there were the motley collection of averages – and worse! In fact, in a way it was a relief to have the first "Terrible"! I can't think of anything worse than having to pussy foot around some appalling guest for fear of them unleashing their venom on a hapless proprietor for something as innocent as putting salt in the sugar bowl! More about Trip Advisor later!

By now I'd managed to keep my anger under control largely as a result of having to serve 13 cooked breakfasts with umpteen rounds of toast and numerous teas and coffees – leaving no time for brimming tempers. That was all about to change though.

At about 9:30, our public school chump thumped his way down the stairs and sat down at a table opposite a fellow alumni. He ran his hands through his dishevelled hair and looked around for the coffee. He was obviously in a somnolent semi drunken state, and perhaps had I realised this then, the next scene would not have happened. Had I realised this, Dr Befuddled would have received a fresh cup of strong black coffee and a Full English to cure the hangover of all hangovers before checking out and making his way back to stockbroker belt. But, I wasn't sitting in front of a laptop thinking calmly and logically about the situation. Instead, I was intensely aware of my pounding heart beat and the slow dripping noise coming from the ceiling next door. Perhaps Dr Slaphappy was still imagining he was in the refectory of the school awaiting a reprimand from his Latin teacher for failing to grasp the pluperfect nominal form of the verb "scribo" when I charged into the room and demanded to see him in my office upstairs. In fact, I said bedroom – his bedroom to be exact – but the effect was just the same! He jumped up to attention and immediately ran up the stairs and into the room like a terror stricken prefect. I pointed to the damp sodden curtains next to the sink and said something about responsibility; by this time, the slumbering ex pupil was fully awake and realising what was happening, and was obviously far from impressed!

I stormed downstairs only to turn round to see him screwing his face up into a pained expression and in a deliberately mocking, high pitched voice saying:

'You've been a very naughty boy: you left the tap running all night!'

No, had he been given a very strong Douwe Egberts, none of this would have happened. He would have been quietly checking the times on his return ticket, wiping the remnants of the egg yolk and Brown sauce from his plate and, perhaps, even thanking me for a lovely stay and even promising to write a glowing review?

Our "prefect" had now fully morphed into the middle aged, respectable professional his privileged education had produced, and he was not happy. All the dressing downs from all the school masters deep down in his subconscious were now bubbling to the surface! All the demands to come to my office at once were dissonant and incompatible with his new found socioeconomic status. He wasn't going to let the proprietor of a guesthouse speak to him like that!

Suddenly, I felt him pushing me backwards, his face directly in mine, and the spittle in the corner of my eye shouting 'NEVER, EVER SPEAK TO ME IN PUBLIC LIKE THAT AGAIN!'

I remember saying to him, 'Take your hand off me!' Luckily, someone finishing off their breakfast in the by now very silent dining room also heard this. I know this because they wrote a very complimentary review detailing this guest's irresponsible and aggressive manner! Over recent years, we've almost become indifferent to reviews – good as well as bad, but this was one I was very pleased to receive!

I think I was too stunned to respond immediately, but our ex public school guest then called me 'A PATHETIC LITTLE MAN!' and suggested I suffered from 'LITTLE MAN SYNDROME!' I remember laughing at these outbursts – much to the annoyance of "Flashman" (as I'd labelled him by then) and pointed out that he no longer went to school and therefore had no reason to be childish! I told him not to be personal and that I'd not used any derogatory comments towards him – even though he was, shall we say, rather rotund! I'd refrained from calling him "fatty" or "tubby" or any of the other nicknames overweight pupils were unfortunately labelled in the bad old days, but there was something about the whole episode which I found very amusing. However, in retrospect I was pleased that I had at least exercised some restraint in this unfortunate unfolding drama!

God knows what he would have done had I called him 'Fatso'!

I think it was my grinning which prompted him to launch into his next phase of attack. Walking into the dining room he informed the other guests that he was a senior reviewer on Trip Advisor and that he would write a damning review on this wretched *Addams Family* like guesthouse before storming off. I opened the front door and wished him a pleasant day.

It didn't take too long for the inevitable review to appear, and I wish I had kept a copy (it was later removed due to a personal attack on yours truly!) as I was really impressed with the quality of his writing – painting a picture of an ogre of a proprietor imprisoned in the bowels of a haunted Victorian dungeon.

I've often re-run the scene in my head where I'm politely escorting him to a table and bringing him a steaming coffee, apologising for the lack of hot water that morning and asking him what he'd like from the breakfast menu. Effective behaviour management is all well and good, and even though I've been on the course and got the t-shirt, sometimes all the theory goes out of the window – especially on a Sunday morning when water is cascading down your living room wall.

After reading this, anyone remotely considering running a guest house will have thrown this book to the ground and be tearing up their letter of resignation. If you haven't done so, then you just might be relieved to hear that this is not a typical guest on a typical night. In fact, this is probably the worst guest we've had in the ten years we've been running the guest house.

The majority of the chapters focus on some of the more humorous and unusual experiences we've encountered, but I thought it only fair to kick off with a horror story to show you that running a guest house isn't about sitting back and waiting for the money to roll in nor is it a panacea for all the problems everyone in paid employment faces on a daily basis.

Having said that, the majority of the "problems" we have encountered along the way have been re-categorized and placed in one of the many "funny" sections – providing the reader with "amusing" anecdotes as opposed to ones of shock and horror.

(I am of course aware that the story of Dr Johns will have shocked many people to the core and obviously would not expect to see anyone falling about in fits of hysterics at this point!)

However, a problem is only a problem if it's perceived as such. Opportunities for growth or development could be an alternative way of looking at problems. I may well owe the Boris Johnson lookalike a vote of thanks. Eastern traditions point out how encountering difficult people in your life enable you to grow and develop as a person. Perhaps I saw something of myself in him? Something deep down in my subconscious that I don't like – and therefore need to change?

Eastern Mysticism aside, some of the most difficult people have also provided me with some the most hilarious, unbelievable and jaw dropping memories to date, so I remain ever thankful to them (including Dr Johns!) and the legacy of laughter they unwittingly left behind as they stormed out slamming the front door behind them.

Chapter 2
Sowing the Seeds!

February Half Term 2006
The first time I thought seriously about running a guest house was during a school holiday. It had been a very long and stressful term. I was so disorganised nothing had been booked or planned in advanced, and the only thing we knew was that we wanted to return to North Devon where we had enjoyed our honeymoon thirty years or so previously.

At the end of a long and tiring journey we found ourselves in Ilfracombe at about 8:30 in the evening with the rain absolutely pelting it down and no obvious place to stay.

Readers will no doubt remember the pre-mobile phone days and, like yourself, wonder how on earth we managed to get things done without being constantly linked to every conceivable restaurant, hotel, garage – in fact anything you'd care to mention on the face of the earth.

The only thing I had to go on was a sign in a window saying "Vacancies". I remember peering out of the misty windscreen up at the row of B&Bs and guest houses. I didn't know what the difference between the two was and at this point couldn't have cared less. The drive from Yorkshire had been a long, tiring one and all we wanted was to find a bed for the night. I pointed up at a large imposing Victorian house with winding steps up to the front door.

'Look, they've got vacancies. Park up and have a look?'

'You pull up and wait here. No point finding a proper parking space if we don't like the look of it.'

I pulled up on double yellow lines, and guessed that at this time of night there wouldn't be many traffic wardens or police about, left the engine running and Jo ran as fast she could, eventually disappearing into the grand welcoming entrance.

It was about 8:35 in the evening. There would be still time for a couple of pints and a bite to eat. I hadn't really felt hungry up to then and was more concerned about finding somewhere to stay for the night. I often wondered why I never bothered to ring up and book somewhere: it would take a lot of the hassle out of going away and there was no excuse now with online booking; press a button and Bob's your uncle. But, then again, I don't like having to drive round with a badly printed map looking for some obscure street, let alone stopping to ask someone directions. I'd often thought about getting a satnav, but liked being in control of where I was driving to and not having to listen to a sultry voice telling me to take the third turn left at the next roundabout. I even get a kick out of sharing survival skills driving down the M1 with Jo, pointing out that we were travelling in a southerly direction as the sun was setting in the west which was to our right. This bemused her ever so slightly as every mile or so was a massive blue overhead sign pointing out that we were travelling South. Jo made some sarcastic comment, pointing out how delighted she was that Ray Mears was in charge of their expedition to chart the unknown coast of North Devon, though hoped nettle tea and boiled seaweed wasn't on the menu…

The satnav is a metaphor for modern life. People acquiesce and give consent for their lives to be controlled and directed in one way or another: 'Turn right for promotion interview; take next left to complete self-assessment targets for appraisal meeting; continue until told otherwise and maintain frugality until payday'. Modern life in a nutshell: following someone else's directions and not having any say in when you stop, start, turn right, left or slam on the brakes and do a full U-turn and screech off into the sunset. North, South, East and West didn't matter anymore. Even with modern technology, we're more lost than ever.

I remember looking up and seeing Jo waving madly from the inside porch signalling for me to park up and bring the suitcases. The reconnaissance party had obviously done its job and soon I was walking up the path to the front door carrying a hold-all with a few bits and pieces for the night.

Jo introduced me to the owners – a friendly middle aged couple. Their collie dog ran around excitedly.

'Take no notice of him, love,' said the lady to both of us, 'He's as daft as a brush.'

'He's lovely!' exclaimed Jo. 'What's his name?'

'Not the dog, love! I'm talking about my husband! The dog's name is Ben. His name is Chris,' pointing to her husband. 'I'm Helen. Welcome to Cliff House. Is it just the one night you'll be staying?'

'Two nights if possible,' said Jo.

Helen presented us with a registration form which we dutifully filled in and handed over.

'Harrogate!' exclaimed Helen. 'Supposed to be posh there! And your accent…that's not Yorkshire is it?'

'No, it's Dutch! But Mike's English. He's from Yorkshire. We lived in Holland for a long time but he's back on home ground now.'

'Ey up!' I added, hoping the hosts would see this as a tongue in cheek gesture and not think of me as a hard done-by northerner with a massive chip on my shoulder.

All smiling and with all the formalities completed, Helen showed us to our room.

'Breakfast is between 8 and 9 o'clock. If you are planning to go out, you'll need the front door key. There's a good pub just up the road and they serve bar meals if you need to get anything to eat. Have a good evening and see you in the morning.'

'Ta very much,' I nodded.

'Stop taking the piss,' whispered Jo.

We made our way up two flights of stairs to Room 6. Jo began the orderly unpacking of her clothes whilst I began sniffing the complimentary toiletries, wondering what they all were for. I never seemed to have much understanding in that particular area. Our bathroom at home was adorned with bottles of all shapes, colours and descriptions though I invariably used the "wrong" one when I washed my hair.

'Couldn't see the label,' I'd say. 'That explains why there wasn't much of a lather.'

Jo started to sort out stuff into neat piles, but I couldn't wait and began to protest; I could taste that first beer and before long I was dragging her down the road towards bright lights surrounding the sign above The Ship Inn.

'A glass of red wine – Shiraz if you have – and a pint of bitter, please.'

I collected the drinks and returned to the table relishing the thought of that first sip of ale. 'Cheers' and welcome to Devon I toasted: we chinked glasses and for the first time all day felt completely relaxed. It had been over twenty years since we were last in Devon. We went there for our honeymoon and had such a great time we vowed to return someday. Well, thirty years on here we were.

'Lovely friendly hotel isn't it? Shame the place we stayed at twenty years ago isn't still around. Still here's to a well-earned break!'

Jo raised her wine glass and I lifted my beer glass, and took a large sip before thoughtfully looking at her.

'Wouldn't it be nice to run a guest house?'

'Where's that come from?' queried Jo. Running a guest house wasn't something she'd really ever thought about.

'Don't know really. Guest houses and B&Bs are something quintessentially British, aren't they?'

'Quinty what?' queried Jo, taking a sip of her wine and noticing I was already half way through my first pint. 'You've finished teaching for a week so you don't need to use the big words now!'

'You know. Typically British or typically English kind of thing. One of the first things you think about when you think of…well, what it is to be English, I suppose.'

'Like fish and chips?' suggested Jo.

'Yeah! Right! Let's see who can come up with the most typical things. First one to hesitate loses! OK you go. I said fish and chips. I give you ten seconds to think of the next one starting…now'

'Last Night of the Proms.'

'Good one. I go Morris dancing.'

'What's that?'

'Blokes dressed up in silly clothes and jumping up and down with bells on their ankles.'

'OK! I'll say strawberries and cream at Wimbledon.'

'Oxford and Cambridge boat race.'

'Carpets in bathrooms.'

'What? That's not typically English or British!'

'It is in my book! You wouldn't find bathrooms in Holland with carpets in. They are hygienic there. Your mum even had carpet running up the side of the bath for God's sake!'

'What about the place we're staying at? Did that have carpet or lino on the floor in the en-suite?'

'Didn't notice. But at least it's got an en-suite! The first time I came to England we had to use a shared bathroom! Remember that?'

'Yeah – we're slowly catching you continentals up. Anyway, I'll let you off but technically that's not quintessentially English,' I said while scratching a 2-2 on the back of a beer mat. 'OK – my turn…and I say the boat race – Oxford and Cambridge.'

'You said that one! Scones and jam and cream…you know… Cream teas! That's it!'

'What about full English breakfast!'

'Something you'd have to cook every morning if you ran a guest house or a B&B,' laughed Jo.

We decided that that was enough excitement for one evening and continued our drinks quietly. I sat back and soaked up the atmosphere of the pub. I was pleased to be able to finally relax. It had been a very long, hard term. I'd been teaching for nearly twenty-eight years and was starting to enjoy it less and less. The bureaucracy, target setting, compulsory lesson planning sheets, Ofsted, mind-numbing meetings and the constant looking over the shoulder. The only thing that didn't change was the kids.

Jo realised that the pressure was taking its toll on me as well. I was coming home late and showed little enthusiasm for anything. The spark had gone out of me. I crawled into bed at ridiculously early times – sometimes as early as 8 o'clock. She knew that this was no way to live a life and she regretted agreeing to move back to the UK if this was the price we had to pay. She knew I was starting to get tired of it; I was bored. Same thing year in, year out. She wondered how long I could stick it, but then decided that we were there for a break and that meant leaving such problems behind for a while.

After a couple of drinks, we made our way back to the welcoming façade of the Guesthouse and up to our room. Jo went inside the bathroom while I jumped on the bed, switched on the TV and flicked through the channels, always intrigued to listen to local news programmes in local dialects. I looked at my watch. Quarter to eleven! I'm normally asleep by this time.

I poured a whisky into a tumbler and picked up the information pack I found neatly presented on the dressing table, skimmed through the emergency fire evacuation procedure (though had there been an emergency I probably wouldn't have remembered where to go or what to do and could only think about Basil Fawlty jumping up and down shouting to his guests that it was not the real fire practice). I flicked over to the breakfast menu. I knew already what I'd have and guessed Jo would go for poached eggs or something quite light. She'd always been more health conscious than me. She was always more adventurous when it came to food as well and would always choose something new and different. It was a standing joke that whenever we had Chinese, I always chose sweet and sour.

'But I like it!' I'd say.

I, on the other hand, criticised Jo for choosing different and obscure things and then she'd get pissed off when she decided she didn't like it and start to pick things from my plate!

I turned the page to discover how to contact an emergency dentist and doctor. St Luke's Roman Catholic service was at 9 and 11 a.m. and there was also a Church of England service at St Mary's at 10:30. That would be something we wouldn't need. I'd been educated at Catholic schools and had had enough of catechisms and creeds to last me a lifetime.

I remember looking at the list of rooms they had in the guest house and the prices they charged for each one and this probably started the ball rolling…

'Two double rooms at £68; two twin rooms at £72; one family room at £78 and a single at £50. I work that out at…'

I rummaged through my bag for my mobile and switched on the calculator.

'That works out at £408 per night. And if all the rooms are full…let's see…that's 365 lots of £408 is…Bloody hell! £148,929.00 per year! Shit!'

'What are you doing now for goodness sake?' queried Jo. 'Can't you leave work alone when you're away?'

'Right. Listen to this; these folk here have six bedrooms, right? If they are full, they get £408 pound a night which adds up to…to a staggering £148,929 a year. Shit, even if they're only half full it's still…'

I fumbled with the calculator and divided 148,929 by 2.

'Seventy four thousand, six hundred and forty five pounds and fifty pence. Christ! Beats teaching!'

Jo was always ready to play devil's advocate and was quick to point out that they wouldn't be full every night, that they'd need to go away on a holiday and, as if that wasn't enough, asked me what sort of eye watering mortgage would be needed to buy somewhere like this in the first place.

Satisfied that this would shut me up, she jumped into bed and opened the book she'd started earlier on in the week. I envied her ability to get lost in a book. It was something I had done easily, but now always had something on my mind; for example, if it wasn't work there was always some other problem ready to jump in and take its place.

I distinctly remember playing with the calculator and scribbling down bits and pieces in the back of a notebook, before the day's driving and the two beers and whisky I'd had started to take their toll on me. I stretched my legs and felt happy and cosy under the duvet. Doing those few sums gave me more than enough food for thought for one night – certainly enough to keep out the list of things I would have to complete for work before returning after the half term break.

I tried to think about other quintessential English things and made a mental list: Ploughman's Lunch, Pantomimes, Coronation Street and Carols at King's College, before moving onto the well-rehearsed ones in which I invariably found myself playing an intrinsic part. Leading Leeds United out at Wembley stadium on cup final day was a favourite, as was lining up with the other fourteen players in a white England shirt for the national anthem at Twickenham before the Six Nations clash with Wales; it always had to be Wales with their fans chanting "Bread of heaven" as this made scoring the winning try with one minute to go before the end of the decider all the more sweeter.

Sometimes I wondered if it was normal to have such day dreams. Psychologists believed it was, though I was aware that my day dreams must be more than simple fantasies and represent deeper longings for something. Freud would have had an answer but there wasn't much place for introspective psycho-dynamic explanations in academic psychology. You can't subject a dream to statistical analysis. Whatever the answer, there'd been no grand plan or anything; it was that bloody satnav again, I grinned to myself.

'Good night, sleep well,' I mumbled. 'See you in the morning.'

7:45 a.m.

Delicious smells of bacon frying permeated the house as I slowly strained my eyes to see the time on the alarm clock.

I turned over to see a space where Jo had been laying and then heard the sound of the shower.

I felt great. There was something utterly reassuring about staying at a B&B. No matter where you were, you felt at home. Everything was cosy about the place, from the friendly owners, the smell of bacon frying and even the sound of the dog barking at the postman. Staying at a hotel somehow didn't give you that same feeling. Hotel rooms were usually cold and impersonal – not that I was an expert at staying at top class hotels. We usually went camping, or rather had done until Jo put her foot down and insisted on going into an apartment for a change. Since then the camping equipment had been assigned to a box in the cellar and I wondered realistically if we'd ever get any use out of it again.

I was excited about the day ahead, though. I was looking forward to leaving the car where it was; had had enough driving the previous day. Time to jump in the shower and get ready for breakfast.

Very soon we were all ready to go downstairs for breakfast. Ben was there to greet us and Helen had to push him out of the way before showing us to the front room where all the tables were made ready for breakfast.

'Would you like to sit here,' asked Helen and pointed to the table next to the window. 'Help yourselves to cereals and fruits and I'll bring you a pot of tea. Or would you prefer coffee?'

'Coffee for me, if that's OK,' said Jo.

'Same for me please.'

We helped ourselves to cereals and bread rolls and sat down at our table.

'Good morning!' announced a tanned sporty guy on the next table. 'Nice day today.'

'Yes, good morning,' replied Jo.

'You from round these parts?' asked the tourist.

'Yorkshire,' I announced.

'Yorkshire!' repeated the tourist. 'Home of the late great Freddie Trueman.'

'Yeah, that's right. In fact, Freddie is buried close to where we live. Often go there for a walk. Frederick Sewards Trueman, English Cricketer is all it says on his tombstone. You into cricket by any chance? Judging from the accent, if you are, it won't be England you're shouting for!'

'I support two teams. New Zealand and anyone who is playing Australia!' laughed the tourist. 'Yeah, over here for a short break looking up family connections going back a few generations.'

Before long, I was tucking into a Full English and Jo, as expected, poached eggs on toast. We continued our breakfast and enjoyed the conversation with the Kiwi tourist, and Chris popped in to have a chat about this and that but mostly the weather.

Jo wanted to pop up to the room so I wandered into the hall and flicked through a few pamphlets of places to see and things to do. I hadn't wanted to see anything in particular. We planned just to walk about and try to remember things from when we were last here in 1984. I thought I might have recognised a few landmarks or buildings on the way yesterday but hadn't. Even the hotel we'd stayed in didn't appear to be there anymore.

'Got a plan for the day?' asked Chris, bringing plates from the dining room for Helen to put in the dishwasher.

'No, nothing special. Just taking it easy,' I replied.

'What do you do when you're not touring about?' enquired Chris.

'Teach – unfortunately,' I replied. 'I'm head of Social Studies at a college in York. And you? How long have you been running this place?'

'Going on ten years now. Helen always wanted to do something like this. I had a full time job and tried to juggle it with cooking breakfasts, but after a while we decided to go full time. Haven't looked back since.'

Mmmm. I went into one of my long deep thoughtful sessions – the type which annoyed Jo intensely when she ever asked me something.

'I've thought about doing something like this for some time now. What advice would you give someone who was thinking of starting up a guest house?'

'Don't!' laughed Chris, 'Bloody hard work. Folk think it's a retirement thing. I did as well but I tell you, I haven't worked as hard in all my life!'

My initial thoughts were that it couldn't possibly be any harder than teaching. I was a hard worker and all my colleagues and management team acknowledged that. What annoyed me wasn't the fact that I had to work hard but that the majority of the things I had to do were wrapped up in mind-numbing bureaucracy and had very little to do with the day to day job of teaching students. Mindless red tape activities dreamt up by bureaucratic twats in Whitehall resulting in bags of shredded confetti and pregnant files full of ill-conceived embryonic initiatives that would be more than likely aborted when some clever politician had thought up a new initiative to take its place. I loathed the word "initiative".

'No seriously,' I said, 'I've thought about it for quite some time now. My wife doesn't want to hear but I'm sort of planning things in the background; getting info together so to speak. If you had some advice, I'd really like to hear it – as long as you don't tell Jo we've had this conversation,' I laughed.

'Three words – location, location, location!'

'I can believe that,' I said. 'This is a great area. I expect you'll have guests all year round. Food for thought anyway. Look, I'd better let you get on with the washing up!'

'Have a good day!'

I picked up a few leaflets and made my way up to the room. Jo was lying on the bed reading her book. She looked up and wanted to know what I'd had been doing.

'Chatting to Chris, the owner'

'What did he say?'

'He was telling me about what it's like running a Guesthouse. You know, the more I think about it the more I like the idea of doing something like this.'

Jo listened. But that's all. She didn't want to think about this at the moment though. We were here to have a relaxing break and not to be thinking seriously about teaching or anything. Certainly not about running a Guesthouse.

'Come on,' she said. 'Let's grab our coats.'

The rest of a week was just what the doctor had ordered for us. We explored all the old haunts we'd been to on their honeymoon all those years ago. We visited Oare church where Lorna Doone was shot by her half-brother Carver while she stood at the altar to marry John Ridd. We wandered around Lynton and Lynmouth, and went on the cliff railway as we had done previously. There was no doubt about it: the break did us a whole lot of good.

I put the trials and tribulations of teaching to the back of my mind which delighted Jo. I didn't mention the word school once. Jo was also pleased I put the nonsense about running a guest house to back of my mind, as well.

Well, at least she thought I had!

Chapter 3
Now or Never!

June 2017

What background music do you play for a group of European vets here in Harrogate for a five day conference on sheep and goats? No, this is not the opening line for a joke! There were three Norwegians, two Germans as well as a Spaniard. They all spoke impeccable English, apart from the poor Spanish bloke. In the end, I chose Manola Sanlucar's Spanish guitar music in the hope that he would feel a little more at home.

It obviously worked, because instead of pointing to something on the menu and grunting he launched into a hundred mile an hour Castilian monologue.

I got the *café con leche* bit without too much of a problem and eventually worked out the *tostada, aceite y tomate*. Our daughter happens to live in Spain so we'd been doing our best to learn Spanish for over a year. I made a mental note I must tell her of this minor linguistic success and then immediately thought how ironic it is that the father who now needs praise from his daughter! We'd been over in Seville and brought back with us a tin of aceite de olive virgin extra from Jaen, so he was delighted when I placed this on the table with a small bowl of chopped tomato.

The Germans asked if they could have breakfast later at 9:00. We informed them that we finished serving at 9:00 and true to form, they returned to the dining room at 8:59 after their morning walk. One wanted an omelette while the other ordered a Full English – minus the sausage – obviously preferring the national bratwurst to the ones supplied by the local butcher.

It was a great booking though it makes you wonder what there was to discuss about goats and sheep over five days!

As the Norwegians were leaving, I asked the one guy who seemed to have a good sense of humour if he had learnt much over the five days. He said he had, so I told him I was going to give him a short impromptu test and asked him how many legs sheep and goats have.

'Four, hopefully,' he replied. 'We did that on the first day!'

Once again we enjoyed discussing the events over the past few days and how interesting it had been hosting these delightful people, although another trip to the tip was necessary with a boot load full of printed material and glossy brochures from veterinary supplies and presentation notes on Dairy goat diseases: signs, prevention and treatment.

Jo recently said that she regularly compares life to how it was when working as a health assistant, coming home with both aching feet and head – not always in that order. This I find highly ironic thinking back to the few months before we finally became owners of the guest house and how Jo finally agreed to join me for the ride.

Christmas 2006

'How to start and run a successful B&B! What's this all about?' mumbled Jo, dropping the festive wrapping paper on the floor and staring at a picture of Mr and Mrs Perfect standing outside a chocolate box cottage.

It was meant to be a subtle nudge, the Christmas after our visit to North Devon – hoping it might help kick start our plans to buy and run a guest house and persuade Jo that it might not be such a bad idea at all.

'First of all it's YOUR plan, not OURS, and it's something I'm not going to think about today of all days,' she replied, putting the book down unceremoniously on top of the Quality Street chocolates.

'Christmas Day of all days, Mike. Can't we give it a rest for at least one day of the year?'

To be fair, I thought I had given it a rest. I'd hardly mentioned the plan to run a guest house since, though I had thought about it a lot! In fact, my notebook was full of jottings and ideas; lists of pros and cons, top ten ideal areas in which to own and run a guest house, and average room rates up and down the country.

Still, at least I'd bought her another couple of main presents and she'd opened them first. The foot massager went down well. She said she was looking forward to soaking her feet and trying it out later on in the day. She was pleased with the toffees, but didn't say anything more about the book. I decided that leaving it in a strategic position on the shelf rather than on top of the chocolates would be a wise move – a more subtle reminder of my life plan.

The big 5-0 was looming around the corner and I was seriously concerned that if I didn't make a major life change soon, teaching up until retirement age would be the only option I had. I'd been working for nearly 28 years, and though my career had had its ups and downs, things were going well for me at the time. I'd recently been appointed Head of Faculty and a Deputy Headship was the next logical step. However, teaching wasn't the same career I'd gone into after university. Increasing levels of bureaucracy and legislation were intolerable. I'd changed too. Despite my youthful looks (so they tell me!) I was rapidly morphing into a grumpy, say it how it is, Yorkshire Man. I'd always been a quiet guy but recently, I had started to air my opinions freely – rather too freely at times for Jo's liking.

'Why do you have to say things like that?' Jo would say to me after a night out with some friends. 'Can't you just relax and have a quiet evening without having to get up on a soap box and tell everyone how it should be done?'

It was rapidly getting like that at work as well. Every new initiative announced, every new governmental strategy was greeted by a "For fuck sake". Admittedly, most of them were mumbles to colleagues whom I knew thought exactly the same. However, as I became more established in the college, I became an unofficial spokesperson for many staff members. Whenever new strategies or initiatives were announced, everyone immediately turned to me to hear what reactionary comments I had to make. Quite often the comments weren't witty or insightful, but just plain vulgar. I realised that this didn't do much for my chances of moving into senior management: yes people and conformists are required for this sort of role nowadays.

I was also becoming a bit of a nightmare for my immediate line manager; he saw me as a maverick, and to be fair, cut me a lot of slack. I'd been allowed to get away with things other members of staff wouldn't have!

I remember the altercation I started with an educational consultant.

The consultant suggested I trial a series of activities with my students to increase their motivation and involvement. It wasn't the activities which caused my heart rate to rise dramatically, but the fact that they were the same type of activities I'd done with students years ago – probably when the consultant was doing his O levels.

'But I was doing that 15 years ago for Christ's sake!' I remonstrated. 'Then "consultants" just like yourself came along and told me not to do it anymore. Told me to drop the airy fairy ideas and get back to basics'

The consultant came out with what I thought to be a load of waffle – trying to wriggle out of the awkward situation I had created.

'Look,' I continued, 'Mike, I know you have a job to do. I know you've been told to spout out this recycled crap by ministers fresh out of Oxbridge, peddling the latest recycled trend. But we spent hours designing and piloting schemes of work like this before they were binned and we were told by Mrs Thatcher and what's his name – Baker or something – to concentrate on the facts and get back to basics. Teach these boys and girls nothing but facts! Didn't someone else write something a bit like that a few years ago?'

Everyone smiled and tittered.

I was furious and struggled to articulate the anger. It put me in a bad mood for the rest of the evening. It was at times like these which made me appreciate what it must be like running your own business; making decisions yourself based on common sense, and not having to chop and change depending on whatever political flavour was currently in vogue.

Jo knew that I was starting to bring more and more problems home with me. I found it hard to relax easily. She'd often call my name and it took two or three attempts to get my attention.

Yes, I needed to do something else; though exactly what, remained the problem.

I was aware this was even affecting my love life; I even shared this with colleagues during an acrimonious meeting when new targets were being introduced. I remember saying that I was heartily sick of the crippling workload dished out by mindless bureaucrats, and no one was more pissed off than my wife whom I was no longer able to satisfy in bed because I was always too bloody knackered. The whole staff room erupted in laughter which probably did more to diffuse the tense atmosphere than fan the flames of insurrection.

Jo remembered one weekend which had been completely ruined. I'd had been accused of calling a girl a "Nigger Bitch!" A parent even threatened to go to the press and call his MP in an attempt to get me sacked! Several meetings were called; governors were brought into school and despite my explanation about the incident, the father was not prepared to listen. In the end, I had to bring my laptop into a high ranking meeting with education officials and show them the clip from the TV series Roots, where the female slave is referred to this obscene, racist and derogatory name.

This had been a particularly nasty incident and I resented the fact that common sense had gone out of the window and a whole series of meetings were necessary to spell out the obvious.

'Would I call a pupil a Nigger Bitch?' I cried. 'Of course I fucking wouldn't! Stupid bastards!'

Though I could frequently laugh away the incidents, this one particularly got to me and left a nasty taste in my mouth. Even after the meeting there'd been no apology and I wondered why I simply accepted such treatment.

Whenever we met up with friends, one of the regular conversation slots would be to ask me what incredulous tales from blackboard jungle I had to relate!

I usually never failed to amuse or astound the group. On the one hand I was grateful for the friends I had and valued their support. However, on the other hand, none of them were teachers and all seemed to be successful, fulfilled, and more importantly, wealthy. I remember recalling one incident when a whole class had accused me of assaulting a girl! The class were feral; unteachable. They refused to follow any instruction. They came into the class charging all over the room, jumping on the tables and chairs, throwing books and equipment all over the show. I grabbed hold of the hood of one of the girls and then it all happened.

The class stood in silence as the girl shouted at me saying that I had assaulted her. She then did something that I had tried to do for ten minutes. She got the rest of the class to sit down at a desk. She gave them all a piece of paper and a pencil and instructed them to write a letter to the head teacher stating that their teacher, i.e. me, had assaulted her.

'You've got to admire her resourcefulness!' I exclaimed to the group of incredulous faces. I explained how I sat down and simply wrote my version of the events, but it wasn't until after several sleepless nights and high level meetings with the senior management team that the incident was finally laid to rest.

I was probably better equipped to cope with the trials and pressures of teaching than many of my colleagues. A maverick attitude, some first rate department members together with the ability to see the funny side of anything, provided me with the necessary resources to tolerate high levels of stress. I'd seen several colleagues succumb to nervous breakdowns and was adamant that I wouldn't follow suit.

I remember one colleague driving to work on the morning of an HMI inspection, and at eleven o'clock was still sitting in the car – his hands frozen to the steering wheel. His wife had to come to school to bundle him in the back of the car and drive him home.

Another teacher was found whimpering in the foetus position under the stairs doing a perfect impression of John Cleese, in the role of Basil Fawlty, having a nervous breakdown – minus the canned laughter, of course! He'd just cracked under the strain and simply couldn't take any more.

How long could any individual continue to tolerate such situations?

Surely, running a guest house was a much more civilised and profitable way of making a living?

Of course, Jo was always eager to play devil's advocate, and used every opportunity available to try to convince me that running a guest house was not the idyllic, stress free occupation I had imagined it to be. I knew that much of what she said was probably true and that she was going to take a lot more persuading before I could convince her that frying bacon and eggs was the right direction to take!

The Quality Street chocolates had long been eaten (except for a handful of strawberry and orange creams), and spring was around the corner before the words "guest" and "house" were mentioned again. This time it was not in the context of buying a guest house, but going for a short break in one; something Jo was all in favour of. She liked the house I'd chosen and was looking forward to spending some quality time together during February half term.

We poured over the photographs of the luxurious rooms on the web site and admired the sumptuous dining room and of course the amazing scenery in the immediate vicinity. I was excited about the break – but excited for other reasons as well. What I had not told Jo was that the guest house we had booked into for our much-needed break was up for sale!

Not that I was in any position to buy it.

It was way above our price range, but I thought that if we liked the experience and got on well with the owners, then, who knows, Jo would maybe start to warm to the idea of co-running a guest house?

February Half Term 2007

The building was a large old rambling Victorian house – the sort that could have been used in a variety of TV and film sets in which a mysterious array of guests arrived for an elegant dinner party only to find that one of them had been murdered and everyone else was a suspect.

We arrived in the middle of the afternoon. The car tyres rolled gracefully over the gravel in the car park and the birds were singing.

'Smell that country air,' I said.

I grabbed the hold-all and, hand in hand with Jo, walked up to the imposing front entrance. Admittedly, we should have been holding an old leather suitcase, but were only staying for two nights – unless the detective forced everyone to stay until the murder had been solved that is…

I rang the doorbell. It was an original bell and not an incongruous buzzer. The tall and aristocratic owner opened the door and welcomed us. So far so good!

'Welcome to Fairfax House', the owner said. 'I hope you have had a good journey. If I can get one of you to complete the guest registration form and then I will fill you in on some of the history of the house before showing you to your room.'

I took the form and began to fill in the necessary information whilst Jo admired the colourful tiled floor and the enormous dresser that filled the entrance hall. She tilted her head back in order to take in the height of the place; the massive beams that hung overhead and the magnificent chandelier hanging from a point too far away to be even seen.

'Well,' the owner continued, 'you are standing in what was a mid-19th century extension to the original building designed and built by the Rev P. J. Fielding. You will notice the ornate wooden carvings above the staircase and we particularly ask guests to take a note of the stained glass in the dining room.'

I tried to appear interested but was distracted by Jo; she stared at me with a look which said 'I came here for a break, not a history lesson!' Unfortunately, the owner didn't see the stone-faced look she gave and continued to enlighten us about the early history of the building.

'The original 18th-century building is our private area but it was built on the remains of an old farmhouse established in the mid-16th century. The floor tiles are original but the tiles above the fire place were brought over from Holland.'

'Isn't it a wonderful building, darling?'

Our host spotted Jo's distinct lack of enthusiasm this time, and shouted for his wife to come and introduce herself.

A grey woman shuffled up and before she got the chance to say anything, our host announced in a Master of Ceremonies manner how he played the eccentric front of house role while his wife was his backbone and the one who really controlled everything.

'She's in charge of the kitchen and the bedrooms.'

Even a fool could work out that kitchens and bedrooms are essentially what a B&B is all about so therefore his wife must have done the lion's share of the work.

'We have a wonderful relationship together. Though we are like chalk and cheese, we make a good team, don't we dear?'

His wife didn't answer. She simply turned around and shuffled back to the kitchen. Jo stared at me in disbelief.

Completely un-perturbed by his wife's indifference, he continued with the "history lesson" and even told us that the wing in which we were staying was haunted by a maid who once worked at the house. Jo certainly could imagine him haunting the house in years to come. He sent shivers down her spine when he was alive; goodness knows what effect he would have on unsuspecting visitors in the middle of the night when he was dead!

We eventually got the key to our room, and Jo let out a gasp of exasperation and wondered how such people could still exist in this day and age. She said he reminded her of Lurch, manservant to the Adams family. The house certainly fitted the bill anyway.

'Did you see his wife?' she asked. 'She simply didn't exist, did she? If that's what running a guest house does for you, then I'm glad we didn't decide to go for one!'

Not the reaction I wanted.

But there were a couple of days and breakfasts ahead; time for her to change her mind!

However, to make matters worse, the first breakfast didn't follow the script I had ordered or imagined either.

'MC host aka Lurch' boomed his good mornings to us as we made our way into the dining room. We were ushered to a table and said good mornings to a tense and uncomfortable couple sitting opposite. We exchanged a few pleasantries before giving our order: pot of tea and two Full English.

When Lurch arrived with the tea he once again began to educate us on the technicalities of pouring it.

'This is extremely delicate bone china. You need to tip it up quite quickly otherwise you will spill everything onto the table cloth'

Nervously, I picked up the tea pot and gingerly began to pour the tea into Jo's cup. Tea began dribbling down the spout, down the fine bone china pot and onto the white tablecloth.

'NO, NO. I TOLD YOU NOT TO DO IT LIKE THAT!'

I uttered an abject apology and held my head in shame. Jo didn't know where to look. She turned to the other nice couple sitting opposite us and they smiled at her both knowingly and apologetically.

We continued to eat our breakfast in stone cold silence and left the dining room as soon as we were able to.

'What a horrible, stupid man,' cried Jo, 'How the hell does he think he can speak to and treat guests like that?'

'No wonder the house isn't exactly brimming over with guests,' I calmly stated, 'I think we'd make a much better go of it than those two sad individuals, don't you?' Seeing an opportunity to spin things around to my advantage, I went on to tell Jo just how much better she was at dealing with people than either of our two hosts.

I think the reply was something to the effect that maybe you are right but I'm pleased I don't have to go on public display every morning like those two sad unhappy and quite pathetic people.

Round two to Jo?

Several weeks, if not months passed by before the words Guest House were raised again in a serious conversation. It was a Saturday morning and I was just browsing through the local paper property guide when I spotted it.

'Jo, Jo, come and look at this!'

We were both immediately impressed by the imposing, eight bedroom Victorian Guest House called Holland House for sale. Jo was Dutch and it was even in our home town as well; this was just too good to be true.

Up until now running a guest house had been my plan. Jo remained completely indifferent to the possibility, though recently she had begun to realise that I needed to do something other than teach. We were settled in Harrogate. We had a bunch of good friends, and the thought of having to leave behind such a good social scene was undoubtedly the main reason why Jo was so against the idea of buying and running a guest house anywhere else. Unlike me, she was happy and content with where she was. Though most of our friends were more affluent, this did not worry her in the slightest. She was pleased for them and couldn't understand why it irked me so much that they were better off. Perhaps it was a male thing? Perhaps it was all down to prehistoric genetic programming and I felt I was coming home each evening empty handed after the hunt?

However, there was something about Holland House which got Jo just a little bit interested. It might not have been the done deal but I could see she was smitten.

We phoned up the estate agent, and at 1 o'clock that afternoon we were knocking at the door of a house which, in several months' time, would become our new home and business.

From that day on, our lives would never be the same again.

Chapter 4
Early Days!

June 2017

We often play Classic FM music on the Hi Fi system on a Sunday morning at the start of breakfast time. It's nice and peaceful and suits the ambience of the dining room when the more elderly guests came down for breakfast (usually the ones who hadn't been out until the early hours of the morning).

By the time the party animals came down at 9:15 or so, Vivaldi's Four Seasons (Spring) and the theme to The Godfather have long since finished and the system had automatically moved on to an upbeat Coldplay album.

However, allowing the system to move on to the following CD is not always a good idea! I remember one morning being in a hurry, and putting something on beginning with an M. What I forgot was that we also had recorded a meditation CD which would automatically follow. As I was rushing between the kitchen and the dining room I wasn't really aware of what was being played until things calmed down (yes, literally!), and while clearing plates was aware of a calm and peaceful voice trying to persuade everyone listening that they were feeling very sleepy and their eyelids were getting heavier and heavier. I should have taken the CD back to the shop as it was not working; everyone was happily chatting, unaware of the subliminal attempts to put them all in a state of somnambulism prior to them checking out and jumping in their cars for the long ride back down the M1.

At first I did the cooking and Jo took care of front of house, but as we got more confident she began cooking – preferring to keep to herself, letting me deal with the myriad of different people and their whims and foibles – at 8:00 in the morning. (If we stuck to plan A, it would have been her and not me confronting our old friend Dr Ed Johns!)

Though she considered herself a good cook, Full English Breakfasts for a dozen or more people was not something she had ever shown any enthusiasm about or any desire to do for that matter. Then there was that awful stuff called "black pudding" which, in her mind, was the most unhealthy, disgusting thing she'd ever heard of – until I told her about fried bread. Needless to say, both items weren't on the menu.

We did have some workers staying with us from the Black Country for several weeks and one of them was addicted to black pudding. I got some for him, but no one else had any. I remember trying a small piece and after five minutes or so, sweat was dripping from my forehead and my heart was beating ten to the dozen; I decided not to touch the stuff again. Even though we don't serve it, many people, after ordering their breakfast will say – 'Oh, no black pudding by the way!'

The early days were very special and in many ways we often wish we had that same level of optimism and excitement as we had then. We didn't manage much sleep during the first night. I even got out of bed at about two o'clock in the morning and wandered about the place just to remind me that it wasn't all a dream.

I asked Jo which was her favourite room, and that the various guide books we'd bought prior to taking over suggested that we should sleep in every room at least once. This was to enable us to see the room from the perspective of a guest and not as an owner. It's only when you stay in a room that you see something that needs attention – wallpaper coming off the wall, chipped paintwork, dripping taps or anything like that.

Any mention of dripping taps or anything to do with water for that matter – and electricity – made me uncomfortable. I read in the book I'd bought Jo for Christmas that any Guest House proprietor would have to have a certain level of DIY ability. I knew that my skills were limited to painting, and that was about it. Even then, I invariably managed to get more paint on me and the carpet than whatever it was I was painting! The theme of water will unfortunately be making a re-appearance later on in the book.

'Oh God, I hope it's a while before we have to start painting and decorating,' protested Jo. 'There are too many flowers and swirls here for my liking. It's all crying out for a bit of neutrality!'

I knew that Jo wasn't the biggest fan of traditional English decor. Carpets in the bathroom were the tip of the iceberg! However, even Jo had to admit huge progress had been made in the UK since she and I first met. However, we both agreed that generally, the decor at the guesthouse was very tasteful and stylish, and there would be plenty of time and opportunity for her to impose her "European" style, whatever that was, in the future.

June 2007

The first night before our first paying guests arrived we simply couldn't sleep and returned downstairs for another glass of wine. The previous owner had advised us to close for the first few days to give us time to sort everything out and get ready for business. Jo saw the sense in this but I was eager to get cracking. Whilst we were the new owners of The Holland House, I was aware that the bank owned half as well!

At 2 a.m., I poured the rest of the wine into two glasses and raised a toast to our new future together.

'Can't believe we've done it,' she said.

'Me neither. Keep having to pinch myself. Cheers and here's to the future.'

'You do think we'll be able to afford it, don't you?' questioned Jo yet again.

I was convinced that we would make a go of the business. I'd never had any previous experience of running a business, but from what I'd seen so far it hardly seemed like rocket science. I had a handful of degrees, including a PhD in Social Anthropology, but decided that running a guest house required nothing more than a good dose of common sense – something that I hadn't seen a great deal of in my day to day work teaching. I was looking forward to rolling my sleeves up and getting stuck into the day to day business of running the place.

Though I had tendered my resignation to the college Principal, I had to remain there until the start of the summer holidays – just over two months or so. We decided that we'd keep on the lad employed by the previous owner; this would ensure Jo wasn't thrown in at the deep end while I was working out my notice. I was on holiday now, and so would get to sample life co-running the place for a week or so before returning to the college.

We both had both spent a couple of days working alongside Margaret, the previous owner, to show us the ropes. I had a small notebook with all the important things jotted down: single sheets were blue edged while the double ones had a red edge. There were notes about marmalades, preferred grapefruit and prune supplies as well as telephone numbers of butchers, laundry services and egg purveyors.

Margaret was no longer there to hold our hands and our first set of guests were due to arrive the following day – English people living in Spain. This is what we were after. Interesting varied people who would enrich our lives with their interesting conversation, tales of intrepid adventure, and dazzle us with their erudition and linguistic prowess.

Well, we were very green.

When the couple eventually arrived, Jo insisted that they complete a registration form. She liked doing everything by the book and was determined that no corners would be cut!

'Estepona, Spain!' she exclaimed excitedly. 'But you're not Spanish, are you?'

'No, English,' confirmed our first guests. 'We're over here seeing relatives, but decided we needed a short break ourselves.'

Jo pointed out where the breakfast would be served in the morning, and brought them up to their room. She wished them a pleasant day and looked forward to seeing them at nine o'clock the next morning when they had requested breakfast.

The following morning, I stretched over to switch off the alarm at six thirty. Jo wondered what on earth I was doing.

'You've got over two hours before you have to start getting ready,' mumbled Jo, looking at the alarm clock display through half closed, bleary eyes.

'Don't worry. Can't sleep anymore; just want to go and make sure everything is ready. I'll bring you a cup of tea later.'

I made my way up to the kitchen and began to prepare myself mentally for the task ahead. Though we said breakfast was served from eight o'clock onwards, and they requested a nine o'clock breakfast, I was already preparing stuff at quarter to seven. Now it takes me ten minutes to prepare breakfasts and the dining room from scratch!

'One small task for man, one giant leap for the proprietors of Holland House!' I tittered to myself.

I was aware of the significance of this breakfast. It would be our first as proprietors of the guest house and no matter what the future would bring, we would always look back and remember 'the first one!'

Having said that, this first breakfast I cooked was one of the most stressful things I'd ever done in my entire life and I'd certainly remember it – although for all the wrong reasons!

To start with, I wondered why it was so stressful and then realised that it was because I did everything myself. Jo was so nervous she just ran around after me pointing out what I wasn't doing correctly: 'The fat's too hot' and 'Did you put salt in the mushrooms?'

The breakfasts eventually left the kitchen and were well received by the expat couple staying in Room 5. Jo was delighted. They were obviously used to dining in style and had developed a cultured European palate, so their stamp of approval was well received by us, two novice proprietors!

After the couple finished their breakfast, we ventured into the dining room and engaged them in conversation – only to find out that they weren't perhaps the sophisticated globe trotters we had initially hoped for.

In fact, the conversation (if it could be called that) was one of the most uncomfortable verbal exchanges I had ever had, and prompted Jo to remind me to tell her just why I had wanted to run a Guest House in the first place.

I began by pointing out that our daughter had studied Modern Languages at university and was working and living in Seville.

'Never been to Seville,' they said. 'Don't think they speak much English there.'

'Do you speak much of the lingo?' I asked.

'No!' was their unequivocal reply, 'most people speak English and if they don't, well, we just shout a bit louder!'

I decided a more open question would perhaps be a better option – giving them the opportunity to open up a little and provide them with the sort of international rapport we had set out to achieve when opening the Guest House.

'What prompted you to move to Spain in the first place?' I asked, hoping their response would touch on some key issues such as the Euro Zone or the Schengen Agreement.

'Too many foreigners over here.' they replied.

I winced. This conversation was going nowhere fast and I was so pleased they were the only ones in the dining room and that their "extreme" comments were not being broadcast across to other customers. I wondered how I would have coped with the conversation had the dining room been full! At the time I didn't realise that I'd get plenty of opportunity to do just that. I decided it was time to abort this abject conversation and told them that hopefully they would continue to be very happy living on the Costa del Sol.

'Can't stand it there!' came their shocking reply.

'Why ever not?'

'Too bloody hot!'

With that, I thanked them for their custom and retired to the kitchen, desperately hoping that our next set of guests would be a bit more like the sort of interesting, cultured people we'd dreamt of welcoming in our Guest House.

Richard was the young helper employed by Margaret, the previous owner. We asked him to stay on – at least until we found our feet. We tactfully decided to give him the first few days off; we wanted to get the feel of the place ourselves and to cook a few breakfasts before our new "employee" worked out that we knew absolutely nothing about running a Guest House!

'I did all the serving and used to make the beds and bring towels up to the rooms. Margaret did all the cooking, cleaning, dusting and replacing stuff,' the new employee cum General Manager informed us on his first day reporting for duty.

'Absolutely fine,' replied Jo, 'but we'd like you to do some cooking as well if it's OK with you?'

'Yeah, but if I'm cooking I'll need to be paid a chef's rate – that's fifty pence an hour extra. Is that OK?'

I nodded, and casted Jo a knowing look. With that, Richard went into the kitchen, made himself a cup of tea and sat down with his laptop – smiling to himself.

'What's the new Wi-Fi code?'

We glanced at each other. It was the first time we'd been anyone's "boss" and we were hardly drunk with power!

'Who the hell does that little smug shit think he is?' whispered Jo.

Later, we reminded each other that it would be in our best interests to keep the peace with him – at least until I finished at the college for good.

'Right, Richard,' I began, 'ready for action?'

Richard was otherwise engaged – dealing with the contents of his "Inbox", and mumbled something to me about being with him in a couple of ticks.

I stormed off upstairs and began stripping the beds.

I always ran upstairs. I saw it as a form of keeping fit. In the beginning, this used to annoy Jo. She thought I was trying to show her he could do more and work at a faster pace than she could. She preferred to take her time and make sure the job was done. She frequently found herself not entirely satisfied with my housekeeping standards!

'Have you finished Room 8?' she'd ask rhetorically.

'Think so,' I would say, knowing full well what was coming. I always thought I'd remembered everything. She had given me a list of what needed to be done in each room; I had a mental tick list and I'd run items through my mind: cups, glasses, bins, tea trays. No matter how hard I tried, I always seemed to get something wrong. This time it was the shower.

'Have you looked inside the shower?'

'Course I did. I cleaned it.'

'Then what's that?' she asked, pointing to a small but never the less discernible curly hair just next to the plug hole.

I peered at the curly little hair in the shower tray in the way a forensic pathologist would scrutinise the one and only piece of evidence remaining after a crime scene.

'Ugh! Is that a…?'

'Yes!'

I muttered something about hairs and something else as well. Jo didn't quite catch it and guessed that she perhaps wasn't meant to hear what I said. To be fair, I acknowledged my shortcomings. I always maintained Jo had a much keener eye for detail than I ever had. A gender issue, maybe? Women on the whole were much better at the micro level, with a keener eye for detail. I was blinded by detail and would rather see the big picture, though at times Jo got a little irritated by the Harvard Business school jargon she claimed I used.

'Broad brush strokes! What are you on about, Mike? Just take the vacuum up to Room 8 please and I'll finish off down here! And take your time! Make sure the job's done well' she'd often say. 'It's not a race!'

But it was just that. It was my way of keeping fit.

'You'd pay forty quid a month to a gym to do this!'

I lost about a stone during the first few months running the guest house. All the running up and down the stairs as well as bending over to make the beds had done wonders for my waistline. Most of the running up and down was unnecessary, however. I would often get to the top floor and remember that I'd forgotten to bring up a new toilet roll. Then after that I'd remember that I'd forgotten a towel or something.

Not that I resented all the extra running up and down stairs. I had always struggled keeping my weight under control, and really enjoyed the physical aspect to my new-found profession. Teaching was far too much of a sedentary occupation: endless sitting at desks or meetings, the temptation of stress relieving snacks at breaks and constant hot coffee from the faculty office next door to my room.

I rarely arrived back home before six thirty, by which time I was only fit to flop in front of the TV and watch the mind numbing assortment of escapist offerings provided for a very undiscerning public.

All in all, in the beginning, I was happy that the rooms took me twice as long as they should have!

The first week as Guest House Proprietors was one of the busiest but most exciting and positive ones in our lives to date.

We went to bed tired, but satisfied!

Chapter 5
The Full English

June 2015

We used to listen to Jack Johnson regularly in order to relax in the evening, but ever since it became Jo's number one favourite to play at breakfast, I can now only associate it with the clatter, hustle and bustle of serving up to 14 people between 7:30 and 9:00. Sorry Jack!

This particular morning we had what Basil Fawlty would have described as Mr and Mrs Neanderthal coming down for breakfast.

They arrived early the previous morning, parking their Mitsubishi L200 2.5 DI-D Raging Bull double cab pickup diagonally across the car park, taking a substantial part of each of the four designated spaces. Jo hadn't noticed when they arrived so it was left to me to knock on their door and ask them politely to move their vehicle. At first they didn't appear to understand me. Both the radio and the TV were on with the volume turned up full. When I finally got the opportunity to ask him politely to move his vehicle, he just shrugged his shoulders and mumbled something about it being a large vehicle and difficult to manoeuvre in such a "diddly squat" of a car park. When I explained that no one else would be able to get their vehicles in, he rolled his eyes and went in to get the keys.

I suppose taking up two full car parking spaces is better than taking up parts of four and decided to leave it at that.

I wrongly predicted that they would be late coming down for breakfast and the classical compilation CD playing at a slightly lower volume than in their room was perhaps wasted on their ears. In fact, it was only when Jo suggested that I went to check if anyone was down that I noticed the pair of them devouring a bowl of fresh fruit salad.

When I say devouring a bowl, I need to explain this in more detail. Every morning I made a substantial bowl of fresh fruit which normally gave everyone a decent helping to accompany their yoghurt or cereal.

This morning it was full to the brim – or it was when I set everything up at 7:30.

Now it was only half full!

I asked them whether they wanted tea or coffee, and returned to the kitchen where Jo thought my impression of two cavemen gobbling stuff into their mouths (or perhaps gobs?) was highly amusing, but immediately put her fingers to her lips when I mumbled something about "greedy bastards!"

I returned to the kitchen with their coffee only to see they had finished their first bowls and had filled them up for a second helping.

Following the script of this unofficial episode of Fawlty Towers, in particular the stage directions in italics, I picked up the empty fruit bowl, took it up to the two refined and polished guests and asked them if they had finished this bowl.

'You did what!' screeched Jo…

Both of them looked up at me in disbelief as if to say what a stupid question – wasn't it obvious that they had finished the bowl of fresh fruit! I muttered something about having to make another bowl and asked them whether or not they'd want a Full English – considering they'd had enough fruit to fulfil their five a day requirement for the next three weeks!

They looked at me in disbelief and without consulting each other, said 'Yep' simultaneously, whereupon I returned to the kitchen and chopped up more strawberries and muttered the satisfying words "greedy bastards" again.

Jo didn't try to shush me this time: she was bent double with laughter, and even to this day, can only see the funny side to this particular incident.

After several weeks running the place, cooking breakfasts had become second nature. At first, I had assisted while Richard cooked the breakfasts. I watched carefully and was soon confident that I could do just as well.

We were pleased that Richard had consented to staying on and working there initially. Jo couldn't have imagined being on her own at first whilst I was working out my notice at the college.

She learnt a lot from Richard and worked hard to keep the working relationship amicable. I was always there at the weekend and similarly tolerated him, though when I returned at the start of the summer holidays, Richard began to find things uncomfortable, and it was not long before he would be looking elsewhere to find his beer money.

For a start, I noticed that he was very slow to get things done; every task was stretched out to last as long as possible. The gaps in between breakfasts annoyed me particularly.

'I could have run up and stripped the beds in three of the rooms between now and the last breakfast,' I'd moan.

It all came to a head one weekend when Richard simply did not arrive to do the breakfasts.

We managed; we had to! But it was not something we would have chosen to do – although in an ironic twist of fate, it did show us that we could cope on our own if we had to.

Richard apologised, and promised he would not let us down again; though the following weekend he did just that! This time there was no phone call though. Now we were on our own!

A Full English is generally the breakfast that is served in a hotel or guest house. It is comprised of bacon, eggs, sausage, tomato, mushrooms, hash browns and baked beans. A chef's qualification is hardly necessary to cook a Full English; it is not the most demanding meal to cook.

The hardest thing would be if a customer requested a poached egg. We've all experimented poaching eggs by swirling the water around to create a vortex for the egg to keep its basic shape and prevent it from dispersing everywhere in the water. This is all well and good when poaching one egg, but a different matter when doing several at a time. We experimented with several ways, but in the end found the poaching pods the easiest way. Technically speaking, this was not poaching but rather coddling. Despite that, it was at least cooked without any fat which is the main reason why many health conscious customers choose a poached egg as opposed to fried or scrambled.

I am not going to insult the reader's intelligence by discussing fried or scrambled eggs.

We offered black pudding at first, much to Jo's disgust. Readers will probably be aware that this is not only limited to this country. In Holland, it is a common dish and called

54

"bloedworst" (blood sausage). Interestingly enough, the majority of customers declined the black sausage and after a while we decided only to buy it whenever it was requested by a customer staying for two days or more.

Apart from that, the secret (if it can be called that!) to a Full English is to cook it as fat free as possible. Grilling, as opposed to frying the bacon, is the best way to ensure this and generally make sure the plate isn't swimming in fat – even though many people do refer to it as a "fry-up".

Sometimes I didn't need Jo to tell me what the order would be.

'Two Full English coming up if I'm not mistaken.'

'Two Fulls please,' shouted Jo, slapping a piece of paper next to me with "2FE" written on it.

Right again! I enjoyed trying to predict what our guests would have. A few weeks as proprietor taught me that stereotyping was not necessarily a negative thing and certain traits could be applied to certain types of people.

Whether or not it was a "class" issue, was difficult to say and I don't propose to examine the nature of the British class system here. There are many clear indicators of class, but as far as I'm aware, eating the Full English isn't one of them!

People who came for a "good night out", which invariably consisted of heavy alcohol consumption, enjoyed a cooked breakfast. In fact, these types of people usually referred to it as a good old "fry-up" – a phrase which Jo did not encourage at all.

She took particular pleasure in ensuring the Full English looked appetizing and appealing on the plate; her introduction of a leaf of parsley on the fried-egg improved the appearance of the dish.

'It needs to look good and not swimming in grease!'

More cultured types, on the other hand, who had ventured to Harrogate to visit the theatre or a concert, were less likely to opt for a Full English and more likely to choose something else from the menu; it might be poached eggs or a smoked haddock omelette.

And then there was the toast; there were definite "white" or "wholemeal" people, and I was usually spot-on predicting who would have what. The same went for ketchup or brown sauce and beans!

'Get the sauces out, this lot'll want brown.'

Slowly, breakfast time became less of a stressful event and something we could actually start to enjoy. There were moments of sheer joy, when a customer decided they only wanted toast – this made life all the easier for me.

Though I felt I could now cook a Full English, Jo decided to enrol us both in a basic catering and hygiene course in order to gain a certificate to proudly display outside the kitchen. Even though I'd completed a handful of degrees during my teaching career, I was secretly worried about completing the basic course. You see, though I had taught all my life, the biggest secret is that teachers actually hate been in the learning role and having people point fingers at them asking questions!

Jo opted to attend the course on a Monday when we had no breakfasts to prepare.

Tea, coffee and biscuits were available for everyone, and the casual introductions began. Been here and got the T shirt, I thought, as I pinned a badge onto my jacket indicating both who I was and the fact that I was the proprietor of Holland House. There were tea and sandwich shop owners, restaurateurs and a couple other Guest House proprietors.

I was pleased to find out that the other proprietors had no guests in either. There was nothing like other owners telling you how busy they were when you were empty!

The initial useful networking session was interrupted when the course leader introduced herself and asked everyone to bring their tea or coffee through to the lecture room.

'That must be Fanny Craddock,' I whispered.

'What?' spluttered Jo, not quite sure if she had heard me correctly in the first place.

'She was the forerunner of Delia and Nigella!'

"Fanny" had plugged her USB stick into the laptop and the objectives for the day were beamed onto the screen overhead.

Oh holy shit! After nearly three decades of teaching, I still struggled to fully understand the difference between aims and objectives. I knew that an aim was an aim and that like all "aims", it might not reach its target (or in this case achieve the objective). In that case, an objective could be likened to a goal but, as Alan Shearer often pointed out on a Saturday night, many goals are also missed!

In-Service Training was something I certainly did not miss. For a start, they were nearly always delivered by consultants, invariably to cascade (a word I hated) information about some new Government strategy or initiative. I always knew that whatever the "new idea" was, it probably had been recycled, but still would require hours and hours of work implementing (another word I hated), writing up new policies and generally having to jump through even more hoops to obtain the funding necessary to implement (sorry!) the changes.

I also disliked the fact that consultants always had to use new, clever "in-words", jingoistic phrases or expressions. I remembered one year when every consultant I knew must have been on a sailing course on The Solent over the summer holidays. Suddenly, all the new terminology used had nautical overtones! The consultants would "tack-into new lines of thought, flag – up issues or simply float some ideas!"

That had been so amusing! People were neither riveted by the course content, nor dazzled by the intellectual process, but were hanging on to every word, simply to see who could spot another nautical reference!

I was half surprised that everyone had dressed up in conventional power suits and were not in pirate costumes complete with earrings, crutches and parrots on the shoulder!

Of course, there were the usual in-jokes with references to nautical characters such as Captain Pugwash and Long John Silver, with less respectful members of staff making sarcastic asides such as "Pieces of Eight" and "Splice the Mainbrace!"

In fact, the only nautical expression not used was the word "sank" – largely because at the end of every session, that's just how I, along with most of my colleagues, had felt.

'Good morning, and welcome to the council's new flagship course on food hygiene.'

'Did she say ship?'

'Be quiet!' whispered Jo.

'As you can see from the course learning objectives, the first thing we are going to do is learn how to wash our hands correctly!'

At this point I started to get a little bit itchy under the collar.

With this, everyone was asked to stand up and pretend to wash their hands whilst "Fanny" marched up and down scrutinising the amateur acting.

Much to her delight, no one was doing it correctly.

She took great delight informing everyone this, and proceeded to demonstrate how to clean between the fingers, the often forgotten back of the hand, and last but not least, the thumb.

This was followed by another excruciatingly embarrassing role play session involving everyone washing their hands correctly, but this time ensuring all the additional aspects of hand hygiene were incorporated into the act. Needless to say, the opposable digit played a particularly active role in the ensuing mime, and a myriad of hitch-hikers, positive re-enforcers as well as good old fashioned thumb suckers took to the stage.

'Thank you very much,' Fanny informed course members in a frosty manner.

Jo thoroughly enjoyed the tongue in cheek role play, though I struggled to see the funny side of it. She told me to loosen up, that I wasn't teaching now and that I was allowed to relax and enjoy things – even if it did involve standing up and making a fool of myself in front of fellow guest house proprietors, and restaurant and sandwich shop owners.

It was also during the course that we were introduced to the "Kitchen Hygiene Pack", which the local council had produced as part of their health and safety promotion. It was a heavy folder, and as soon as I picked it up, I decided that carrying it home would be a health and safety issue in its own right.

Our attention was brought to the different sections of the pack, but we were specifically asked to look at the food preparation and cooking section.

More heavy sighs and rolling eyes followed.

"Fanny" informed everyone that after each food preparation and service, the council required owners to complete a tick list of the things that they had done both before and after the service, as well as a damage limitation section that involved completing an incident sheet if anything went wrong.

I mumbled something to myself and checked my watch to make sure that it wasn't the First of April.

After requesting further clarification, the lecturer pointed out that it was all very straightforward.

'Well,' she said, 'suppose you had put some sausages in an oven or frying pan and cooked them prior to serving. If you took out a sausage and noticed it wasn't cooked properly, this would class as the "incident", and so, on the form you would fill in: took sausage out of pan or oven and noticed that it was not cooked completely.'

She then asked everyone what action we would be necessary to take to ensure the sausage was cooked completely before serving.

Whilst Jo was diligently making notes, I was starting to show observable signs of acute discomfort and soon the giggling became contagious.

'Put it back in the pan,' someone shouted.

'Exactly!' exclaimed the lecturer.

'Ah, but what if the sausage had been cooked in the oven?' shouted someone else trying to look as though he was taking the course seriously!

We were then told that the correction to be taken would be to put the sausage back in the pan or oven and on the form, under where the incident had been logged we would complete the section ACTION TAKEN – filling it in, indicating that the sausage had been put back in the pan or oven to ensure it was completely cooked before serving.

Eyes really began to roll at this point, but as Jo correctly informed me, I wasn't the teacher now and I should take things more seriously as I was never too old to learn something new.

We returned home proudly holding a certificate to prove we now had a basic hygiene certificate. Yippee, I knew how to wash my hands!

Unfortunately, we also brought home the large hygiene pack with a generous supply of daily forms to be filled in and wondered if breakfast would taste any better the next day.

To be fair, we completed the form religiously for about two weeks. Of course, the problem that sprang to mind was what should be done with the completed forms?

Jo told me that she had read somewhere that we were legally obliged to keep everything for seven years. That meant that if we provided a cooked breakfast every day, I would need to store around over two and half thousand sheets of paper.

'That couldn't be right, could it?'

The answer to my dilemma came from a seasoned hotelier at a small hotels and Guest House Association coffee morning. This is a useful platform for meeting other Guest House owners, exchanging stories and anecdotes, and discussing pressing issues such as online booking systems, laundry rates and Star rating systems.

It was our first meeting and so we were anxious to meet other proprietors and hopefully glean some useful tips and advice.

'Can I have your attention everyone? This is Jo and Mike from Holland House; they've taken over from Margaret.'

There followed a series of waves, smiles and general welcomes from a group of unfamiliar faces.

I noticed a group of blokes in a corner laughing and sharing a few jokes about something and decided that I should slowly move over and introduce myself.

'He's bloody useless. Should have sold him to Everton when we had a chance.' exclaimed one of the blokes in a thick North East accent, and immediately I was relieved to be standing with a group of "normal" people who talked about things other than the best way to poach an egg!

'Hi, Dave from The Green Dragon. Pleased to meet you. How's it going?'

'Great thanks! Bit of a steep learning curve but getting there.'

Introductions were made and now I knew the owners (well, the male half of them anyway) of four other guest houses in the area. After plucking up the courage, I pointed out that we had just attended the hygiene course and told them about the "pack" we had been given. I mentioned the compulsory daily incident sheet which was an integral part of the pack.

'Do any of you use the pack?' I asked, trying to look as indifferent as I possibly could but in fact ready to pounce and hold onto every word they said.

'Fuck Off!' was the unequivocal reply from all four blokes who rocked with laughter in unison.

I continued to relish the conversation about Sunderland's prospects of remaining in the Premiership for the remainder of the season before returning home and emptying the entire contents of the health and safety file into the waste paper recycling bag!

Health and Safety 0 – Sunderland 1!

Chapter 6
That Was the Week That Was!

May 2008

One of the reasons we were so excited about our new adventure at Holland House was the opportunity to attract more European visitors. We have family and friends in several countries across the continent.

We had translated chunks of the web-site into German, French, Spanish as well as Dutch, and sat back and waited for the phone to ring and prepare for people from varying eclectic backgrounds to visit us and enrich our lives with their erudite tales and allow us, in return, to share our love of this incredibly rich and varied area of North Yorkshire.

We soon came to understand where most of our custom came from and to give you, the reader, a clue, it wasn't The Dordogne, Bavaria or the Alps: most of our visitors came from Newcastle.

Our first real European visitor resulted in the most stressful week of running the guest house to date and brought us down to earth with a real thump.

I remember I had just about finished changing the bedding in Room 5 when I heard the telephone. It continued to ring so I rushed downstairs to grab the phone. Chances were it would be someone cold calling – offering to give us a better electricity or gas deal. If not, it would be someone wanting to talk to us about web site optimisation and the best way to achieve a higher ranking on the Google search engine.

I remember one morning when we had been plagued by such nuisance calls and in a fit of desperation, I picked the phone up when it rang next and screamed 'what do you want!?!'

A quiet and timid voice answered 'I'd like to book a room please.'

Ever since, I was more aware of the possibility of potential guests phoning and so I picked up the phone and answered in a polite and business-like manner:

'Good morning, Holland House. Mike speaking.'

I struggled to hear most of what the gentleman on the other end of the line said, but the gist of it was that he and his partner wanted to stay for two whole weeks!

I took down the necessary information, thanked the gentleman for his booking and informed him that I was looking forward to meeting him in a few weeks' time.

'Jo! Jo!' I yelled from the top of the stairs. 'Room 4 booked for two whole weeks!'

This was really fantastic. A two night booking was considered a good one. You don't have to strip the bed the next day and so got two nights for price of one laundry strip. But fourteen nights! Two whole weeks was incredible.

Many guesthouses don't even accept "one-nighters" as they are called in the trade. They think that having to strip a bed and clean a room after just one night is too much trouble. They tend to be the settled proprietors though – the ones like Margaret who have paid off their mortgage and are almost running the place more as a hobby than a serious business. We had a big mortgage, and as far as we were concerned, seventy quid was seventy quid.

'Did you charge him seventy quid?' continued Jo.

'No. I thought for two weeks it was a bit steep so I said we'd do it for £55 a night. He arrives in a month's time. Good, eh?'

'What did he sound like?'

'Hard to say, but I think he's a bit… Eccentric.'

I stormed off upstairs at eighty miles an hour only to remember I'd forgotten the toilet rolls when I got to the top!

At this point you may well be thinking what the significance of this booking was, but the day our long term guests were due to arrive also happened to be the arrival day of our first visitors from Germany.

They had emailed Holland House to enquire about our Guest House and the possibility of staying here for a few days. They were very excited about visiting Yorkshire and in particular about visiting "Mike and Jo's beautiful house".

All in all we were really enjoying life at the helm (excuse the nautical reference) of the guest house and were especially excited about the week when our German guests, as well as the long term guests of course, would be arriving.

I had been working down in the cellar (as usual) when the long term guests arrived. I ran up the stairs eagerly to greet them, but was stopped in my tracks by a very discernible and unpleasant odour that permeated the whole hall. I tried to ignore the smell – dismissing it as something that had blown in from the fields and welcomed the guests to Holland House.

As we were exchanging pleasantries, I could not fail to notice the large stains on the lady's coat. I tried as hard as I could to avoid staring at her, but as a result noticed that the man's face was covered in huge black heads as well.

'This is Mary, my girlfriend and we're going to get married next year, aren't we darling.'

I stared at the two guests in disbelief. Surely these weren't the people who would be staying with us for two whole weeks?

'Yes…welcome,' I stuttered. 'Can I get one of you to complete the guest registration form, please?'

The male guest picked up a pen and stared at the piece of paper. 'Do I put my name here?'

'Please,' I responded – not quite sure how this was going to develop.

Slowly, the male guest began by writing his name in huge block capitals taking up nearly half of the form. 'It'll be easier if I let you write the rest in' and dictated to me their address and telephone number.

It was not an ordinary address, and by now I'd already worked out that it was probably some sort of sheltered accommodation. But already, from our few brief exchanges in the hall, it was obvious that there was no way that these people were either independent or capable of looking after themselves and loud warning bells were ringing in my head.

'I'll give my wife a shout. She'll want to meet you!'

With that, I yelled at the top of my voice and a bewildered Jo appeared at the top of the stairs wondering what all the commotion was about.

'Come and meet our new guests, darling! Sorry, I didn't catch your names?'

'I'm Mary,' replied Mary.

'And I'm Peter.'

'Welcome to Holland House' replied Jo, wondering why I was lifting my nose in the air and tilting my head towards the two guests.

'Mary is my girlfriend. We're going to be married next year.'

'Oh, congratulations!' said Jo, looking at me somewhat confused as though she was missing out on something and I wasn't giving away any of the clues.

'Yes, congratulations…let me show you up to your room. I'll…I'll bring up the cases for you.'

I attempted to lift the grubby suitcase and my arm locked immediately. Although I enjoyed the physical challenge of running a guest house, trying to pick up heavy suitcases was not one of the Olympic sports I would have signed up for. I'd already had a few back problems and was always careful when it came to lifting anything heavy – and God was this heavy.

'What the hell have they got in here?' I muttered to myself. The optimism I'd woken up to was vanishing rapidly. There was an uncomfortable, very discernible waft of B.O. in the air and to make things worse, the German couple were due to arrive within the hour.

I reminded myself of their email and something about 'looking forward to staying in your lovely house!' Well, up until half an hour ago it was a lovely house. The scent of the fresh flowers and furniture polish was everywhere; now it was BO.

After depositing the bag of dumbbells in their room, I immediately set up an incense burner in the corridor. We had a whole array of different aromas and I rummaged through the basket of small bottles before deciding upon Dewberry. I quickly lit a tea light under the incense burner and added several drops of the essential oil before putting in a few more in for good luck.

After a short while, the incense seemed to be doing the trick and all normality was resumed. Or at least that was what I thought!

The two charming, intelligent German guests arrived and were greeted by a rather nervous owner when they rang the front door. They both spoke impeccable English. A few pleasantries were exchanged and I took them to their room. They were not disappointed by Holland House but probably wondered why I was sniffing the air all the time.

At breakfast the next morning, Peter and Mary were down at 7:30 waiting outside the dining room. I got a shock when I opened the door to see them 'lurking' there and, once again, the sickly BO smell permeated throughout the entire hallway.

'I'm off out for a fag,' Mary informed her boyfriend.

'Would you like tea or coffee?'

'Pot of tea for two please!'

I returned to the kitchen punching the air muttering to myself.

'They're both down and they both stink!'

'Try to keep a lid on it Mike; they are both paying guests. We'll try to sort things out later when we go up to their room.'

I could not wait!

Jo returned to the dining room with a pot of tea.

'What are your plans for the day, then?'

'We're off to Leeds market, aren't we, love,' replied Peter, as his girlfriend returned to the dining room, this time wafting of stale nicotine.

'Oh that's nice,' replied Jo, grateful that Mary at least had gone out to have a smoke.

I prepared the two Full English breakfasts with beans, brown sauce and white toast for Peter and Mary whilst the two German guests made their way into the dining room.

'What a lovely room,' uttered the couple as they ventured into the dining room. They looked over to Peter and Mary and wished them good morning.

'The Germans are down, but I don't think they have noticed anything; if you don't get close to them you can't smell anything.'

The rest of the breakfast passed without incident, and soon Peter and Mary returned to their room to prepare for their day at Leeds Market.

After breakfast, Jo wished everyone a pleasant day and set about her daily routine. I normally went to strip and make the beds of guests checking out but this particular morning I made a direct line for Room 4 to see what sort of a state the "engaged" couple had left it in.

What greeted me was a scene more reminiscent of a war-torn Lebanon or a squalid Delhi slum. The smell – no, stench – was overbearing. In the middle of the floor was an electric heater which had been left on full blast with five completely sopping wet towels on top. The bed was sopping wet too, and to this day neither Jo nor myself got to the bottom of what had gone on in that room the previous night; we probably did not want to know either.

Most of the day was spent getting the room dried out and presentable, though even by mid-afternoon the damp patch on the carpet was still quite noticeable and the stale stench seemed to be irreversible.

The incense burner was brought into the room and I decided to leave the windows wide open – at least until the guests returned later on that day.

I spotted the grubby suitcase on the floor next to the bed and couldn't resist having a peep. After all, how could any single item of luggage weigh as much as that?

I peeped inside and was shocked to see that it was completely full with cans of Coca Cola! I could not believe what I had just seen! One or two cans in the room were the norm and quite acceptable for couples to wind down after a tiring sightseeing day with their favourite tipple and a coke. But a whole suitcase!

The rest of the day was spent finishing off the house and servicing all the rooms that had been taken. Our normal routine had been to go out for a walk – perhaps to a cafe for a coffee and piece of cake, but on this particular day we decided not to venture out at all; we were exhausted.

We also wanted to be on the premises when the mysterious couple returned from their outing to Leeds market.

Eventually the peace and calm was disturbed when the two dreary visitors returned. We wasted no time in pouncing on them and demanding to know what on earth had gone on in their room the previous night and why all the towels were so wet.

'You what?' replied Mary.

'Why was the room such a mess?'

'Don't know,' they replied, like two naughty school children who daren't look their teacher in the eye.

'You must know,' I stuttered, 'you can't have let the room get into such a state without knowing why!'

After a moment of pondering, Mary looked up at me and said, 'Sorry!'

'It won't happen again, will it, darling,' promised Peter and once again the fusty smell of BO returned. I escorted the couple to their room, and discretely and quietly took the incense burner out. The room did smell a lot better, but now that they had returned, the stale smell of their dirty clothes seemed once again to permeate every nook and cranny of the entire building.

'You can still smell them!' I protested to Jo.

I brought the burner downstairs and lit another tea light. I searched for the Dewberry and realised that the whole bottle had been used in Room 4. Ylang-Ylang! That would do.

On the label it read that this particular aroma was helpful with anxiety, tension, shock, fear, panic, rapid breathing, rapid heartbeat, aphrodisiac, physical exhaustion, frigidity, impotence, insomnia, depression and stress. Give, or to be more accurate take, a few of these symptoms, I decided that this one fitted the bill and emptied nearly an entire bottle into the water.

Two days later, we'd had not only used up the Ylang-Ylang, but had finished off the Frankincense and Patchouli as well.

We wondered just how it was possible for the German couple to stay for several days without batting an eye lid (or to be more accurate – twitching a nostril), and they left smiling and happy after having a delightful stay and left wonderful comments in the Holland House guest book:

Bremen Osterholz
Thank you very much for the warm welcome, delicious breakfasts and lovely room. Harrogate is a lovely place and a very good starting place for wonderful days out in the Dales, especially Bolton Abbey! Hope to see you again, maybe in Fischerhude near Grasberg?
Thank you! Auf wiedersehen!

Again, at half past seven the next morning, Peter and Mary were standing outside the dining room. Jo opened the door and ushered them in – noticing the sour reek oozing from the both of them.

'How do you go about washing your clothes while you're away for so long?' asked Jo.

'Don't know,' came the reply.

'Well, I tell you what. Put all your washing in a plastic bag and bring it downstairs before you go out for the day and I'll see what I can do. OK?'

'Thank you,' replied Peter, 'isn't that kind, Mary?'

'Yes.'

Once again, I prepared the Full English complete with beans, brown sauce and white toast. Jo served the meals, though persuaded me to bring the toast and collect the empty plates when they had finished.

'Hope you enjoyed that!' I smiled, happy that Jo had made some headway towards solving the problem of the stench in the Guest House. 'Have you any special plans today?'

'Yes. We're off to Leeds market. Mary likes it there, don't you, love!'

In fact, apart from one trip to visit the Railway Museum in York and a half day bus trip to Skipton Castle, every day was spent at Leeds Market. There is no doubt that a visit to Leeds is incomplete without looking inside the indoor market with its amazing Victorian architecture and the very eclectic, diverse range of stalls to examine. Occasionally, on a quiet day, we'd have a drive over and stock up on fresh fruit, though after a couple of hours I had seen nearly everything there was to see and that was after rummaging through the second hand books!

Our guests' obsession with Leeds Indoor market needs to go down as one of history's greatest mysteries!

Jo's astute move of offering to wash their clothes together with their pro-active damage limitation strategy (together with several cans of air freshener) kept the room free from further damage during the rest of their stay at Holland House.

I had to go up to their room several times and plead with Mary not to smoke in the en-suite. She looked rather perplexed and even questioned me – wondering how on earth I worked out that she had been having a crafty fag on the loo with the window wide open.

In fact, Jo had spotted her, returning from the Cash and Carry on a couple of occasions – almost dangling out of the window in her desperate attempt not to set the fire alarm off. If that had not been enough evidence, there was also the pile of ash and cigarette ends on the path immediately below their window.

Gradually, the supply of Coca Cola diminished and before too long, the suitcase was completely empty and it was time for the couple to pack their things and prepare to depart.

As usual, at half past seven on their last morning, they stood outside the dining room waiting for me to open up.

'Good morning, Mary! Good morning, Peter!'

Had Jo been around, she would have chastised me for sounding so happy and enthusiastic.

'Pot of tea for two, is it?'

'Yes, please, and the usual – Full English with beans and a round of white toast.'

'No problems – coming up shortly!'

I made my way to the kitchen only to turn round to find that Peter had been following me.

'Mike, I'm sorry about the trouble we have caused you,' he whispered, 'we are very grateful to you and Jo for all you have done for us.'

'Don't be daft,' I replied, taken aback by the sudden outburst of remorse. 'We've enjoyed having you. It's been an interesting and eventful stay!'

The couple devoured their breakfast and even asked for more toast. They made their way upstairs to collect the rest of their things while we cleared the dining room.

We ought to have been pleased that our guests were finally leaving though for some reason, there was a tangible sadness in the air, a distinct melancholy.

We slowly cleared away the dirty plates, cups, glasses and cutlery.

Before long, the clumsy dragging of bags along the corridor above and then the inevitable bumps as they descended the staircase could be heard.

'Right, we're off now. We'd like to thank you both for making our holiday so special. You have really helped us.'

'We really haven't done anything special!'

'Oh you have. You don't know. We don't meet that many kind people, do we, Mary?'

'No, we don't,' added his girlfriend.

'And,' Peter added, 'we're sorry for all the problems we caused you and hope you aren't too mad at us. Oh, and thank you for doing all our washing as well.'

'Oh, that was the washing machine, not us!'

'Well, we're off to the station now to catch our train. If we don't get a move on we'll miss it, won't we, love?'

'Good bye. Thanks for your custom!'

The couple turned and walked out of the entrance and down the steps to the road. Thankfully, Mary's bag weighed considerably less than it did when she arrived. I stared at them as they walked down the road arm in arm, and my eyes welled up with tears.

'You live and learn, don't you?'

'Poor people,' said Jo.

'Were these the best guests we've had or the worst?'

'I keep telling you that you learn from everyone. What does the Desiderata say? Listen to others, even the dull and the ignorant; they too have their story.'

I sat thoughtfully for a few moments before leaping into action.

'Right, bleach and air freshener! Come on – let's hit Room 4!'

Chapter 7
Drips, Leaks and Self-Sealing Coupling-Connectors

This particular Sunday morning, the classical CD compilation had played out and I put on The Hollies' Greatest Hits. The group had been playing at the International Conference Theatre the previous evening, and the majority of the guests staying with us had been to see them – including the group of six ladies from the three twin rooms.

They'd all had a great time and thanked us both for a lovely stay, asked for a business card in case they were to come back to Harrogate again (the Hollies have played here at least three times since we've been at Holland House) but before they went, one of the ladies said – and this is the bit guest house proprietors don't like because it's invariably going to either be a minor criticism such as there was only one cup in the room or it would result in me having to do some minor (or in some cases major) DIY work!

'I need to mention, there appears to be some sort of leak in the roof; I think it must be due to the awful weather we've had over the last few days. Hope it's not too much of a problem! Bye!'

I tried to smile at the three ladies as they made their way down the steps, but the sickening knot in my stomach was nothing psychosomatic and I knew it would not go away until the leak had been sorted. I charged upstairs, and to my mild relief, found nothing more than a small trickle coming along one of the beams in the very top room.

'Once the rain stops, it'll be alright,' I muttered to myself, ever the optimist.

Sundays were always the busiest day of the week. Whatever business had been like during the week, Saturday nights were invariably full, and as most people checked out the following day, it meant we had to break the Fourth Commandment, to remember the Sabbath day, and to keep it holy!

The rain had stopped outside but, unfortunately, it was not the case in the family room; if anything, the leak was gaining momentum.

This was not what I wanted to see; the knot in my stomach tightened even more. I eyed the loft access and knew that the time had come to face my fears. I went downstairs to fetch the ladder and prepare myself for an uncomfortable – and probably wet – afternoon.

'Where's the torch? Anyone seen the torch? Fucking typical! You can never find a torch when you really want one.'

I eventually found a small flash light which, Jo pointed out, had been attached to my key ring for about a year, and after much huffing and puffing made my way into the loft – careful not to put my clumsy foot through the ceiling of the room below.

I didn't even have to shine the light around to find out where the leak was coming from; I could hear it. The pipe attached to the storage tank was badly corroded and water was hissing uncontrollably from a crack in the bend.

'Oh fuck! It's a leak from a pipe going into the water tank!' I shouted to Jo, standing in the room below.

'What are you going to do?' shouted Jo, from the relative warmth and comfort of the room below.

'I don't know, but think I can sort it out temporarily!' After a calming down and telling myself that I just needed to apply a bit of cold logic, the problem should be solved. The room was not taken for the next three days, so there was plenty of time to sort it out once and for all.

'I'll try and turn this valve; see what happens.'

The hissing increased and before I could say Niagara Falls, my face and whole upper body was soaked through as water began spraying everywhere.

'Mike, what's happening?'

'FUCKING HELL! Fucking water, fucking everywhere!'

'What did you just do?'

'I know, I know!' I screamed at poor Jo standing helplessly at the foot of the loft access.

In a desperate attempt to solve the situation, I instinctively turned the valve in the opposite direction. EUREKA! The water gradually spluttered to a complete standstill and I breathed a huge sigh of relief!

There was no getting away from the fact that anything to do with water, showers or bathrooms was an area with which I was very uncomfortable with.

Yes, I'd read Zen and the Art of Motorcycle Maintenance, and knew that I should start to understand the basics of plumbing (as opposed to motorcycle maintenance, of course), if only to save Holland House a great deal of unnecessary expense.

I had tried to do things myself – despite the advice to the contrary from fellow guest house proprietors.

A quick call to the emergency plumber and a couple of hours later, all was well and, more importantly, dry. Despite having to write a cheque for a few hundred quid, I was a happier (and drier) proprietor.

Holland House had a total of 11 toilets, 9 showers, 2 baths and 13 sinks, so as far as water was concerned there was a vast array of things that could go wrong – and frequently did!

We had only been there several months when we noticed an obnoxious smell every time it rained and we presumed it was the drains. This was not what we wanted. We called out someone to check the drains, and surprisingly he confirmed they were all clear, which made us even more confused.

What on earth could have been causing such a dreadful stink?

The answer came after a short discussion with a neighbour after I mentioned the problems we'd been having – or thought we'd been having – with the drains.

'You're living in Harrogate!' he said, 'and these properties sit on one of the largest sulphur reservoirs in Europe!'

I felt slightly embarrassed that I hadn't considered this, and of course, when we thought about it, the rotten egg smell should have been the obvious clue!

We were embarking on a journey which would throw many lessons on our path; some lessons could be ignored or solved with a fat check made out to a plumber, but there were times when I knew I would need to man up and face my nemesis head on! Such an occasion came just before one Christmas holiday,

x

when guests in the same room that had the leak complained about the power shower, saying that it was not working. I put the shower on, and after standing for ten minutes with my arm under ice cold running water, eventually came to the same conclusion as the guests. On Christmas Eve, the chances of getting a plumber were small and the chances of getting a cheap plumber were absolutely zero, which meant that I would have to do the job myself.

I remember the fateful trip to the DIY store to buy a power shower. I'd noted down every detail of the old shower in the naïve hope of buying an EXACT replacement. I scoured the shelves and picked the same brand as the old one.

Well, I thought it was the same brand.

'Is everything I need in here?' I asked at the checkout.

'Just follow the instructions and it should be self-explanatory.'

I paid and jumped in the car, preparing myself for the DIY equivalent of scaling the north face of the Eiger. Instead of carabiners, crampons, ropes and a harness, I had a screwdriver, drill, wall plugs and a hammer.

I stood at Base Camp, or to be more precise, the foot of the stairs and stared upwards to the fire door which gave access to the second flight of stairs ascending to the second fire door and the final steep ascent to the family room.

I had, of course, remembered to turn both the electricity and water off at the mains, and began climbing up towards unfamiliar cold, wet territory.

The shower came off quite easily, though I shuddered at the sight of three thick, threatening, power cables sticking out of a hole in the tiles with a DANGER sign written in large red lettering all over the back of the old shower unit.

'Fucking hell! What the fucking hell have I fucking started?'

For a minute, I began to even feel slightly confident – thinking that I might have even cracked this DIY business once and for all. I managed to put the shower in place, but the optimism drained as fast as a one-handed abseil back to BASE ONE when I realised I could not connect the shower unit to the water mains.

The water attachment at the back of the new shower did not match the one on the pipe sticking out of the hole in the tiles. For the second or third time that day, the knot returned to my stomach and I jumped into the car and drove round to the DIY centre and marched straight up to the Customer Service Section.

I took a deep breath and told the man with a "Here to help you" t-shirt on behind the counter, 'Sorry to bother you, but I purchased this shower earlier on today and despite being told that it was straightforward and everything I needed would be in the box, it turns out that it isn't because the water bit at the back won't connect to the water pipe thing sticking out of the wall.'

'You need a fifteen millimetre, self-sealing, coupling connector,' replied the man who was there to help me.

'A what?'

'A fifteen millimetre, self-sealing, coupling connector.'

'Yes, I know. I heard you first time. These fifteen millimetre, self-coupling things – can you buy them here?'

'No. You need a plumber's merchant store for that.'

'But I was told everything I would need was in the box!'

'That includes the instructions, sir, and if you had read the instructions carefully, you would have realised that you would need a fifteen millimetre, self-sealing, coupling connector.'

I stormed out of the DIY store and made my way to the only plumber's store I knew in Harrogate.

'A fifteen millimetre, self-sealing, coupling connector, please; a fifteen millimetre, self-sealing, connector, please; a fifteen millimetre, sealing self-coupling connector, please.' I repeated – for fear of forgetting something small yet so important.

The car screeched to a halt outside the plumber's merchants. I slammed the door shut and charged into the store still practising the, by now, irrelevant list of words I'd had been trying to remember by heart.

Time stood still in the old shop. A clock hanging on the wall ticked in an accurate, routine manner; an old-fashioned smell of Swarfega filled the air, and I waited for Ronnie Barker, dressed in his brown coat, to come to my aid.

I reminded myself that it was not fork handles I required, but a fifteen millimetre coupling self-sealing connector hoping that the man in the brown coat behind the counter (surely he had to be wearing a brown coat?) was not going to ask me any further awkward questions or say something like, 'We've only got a twelve millimetre,' or 'Do you want a mark one, two or three version?'

To my delight, a young bloke wearing jeans and a t-shirt did not even flinch when I mumbled out what I had been trying to memorise by heart for the past twenty minutes or so, and his hand went straight to a drawer, pulled out a small packet, slapped it on the table and in the usual macho manner that seemed to be the norm in such a "man's man" type of shop said in a similarly no-nonsense manner, 'Four pounds sixty, please.'

I gladly handed over the cash, and thought to myself that if it meant that the shower would be safely installed that evening, I would have gladly paid several times that amount.

The shower was installed that afternoon and no one was more surprised than me when it actually worked. I felt extremely satisfied and contented with life in general, having overcome my worst fears; I could not remember ever coming home from college with such a sense of achievement.

Although my teaching days were over when I left the college in York, a year or so after taking over the running of Holland House, I was asked if I could do some supply teaching at a nearby school.

The money was useful and I was free at weekends to jump back into the role of guest house proprietor. It also gave me the opportunity to reassess my decision to leave the profession to run a guest house and to compare the respective merits and drawbacks of each job.

Sociologically speaking, occupations are one way of determining class status in modern Britain, and according to the National Statistics Socio-economic Classification Scales, teaching is ranked at 1.2 on a one to eight scale – eight being the long-term, unemployed dregs of society sort of people.

Guest house proprietors, unlike teachers, are not cited in the examples used to illustrate categories. This is probably because running a guest house as a profession is hard to pin down in any specific category. Me, on the one hand, owning a large guest house demands some level of managerial expertise, inter-personal skill and marketing knowledge, and would probably rank high on any classification scale. However, many of the physical tasks associated with running a guest house would be ranked fairly low on the same scale: frying bacon, making beds and ironing quilt covers; though it is doubtful if there could be a task lower than cleaning toilets.

Job satisfaction, opportunities for further development or promotion might not figure highly on your typical toilet cleaner's profile but to me, there was something strangely therapeutic about cleaning loos – especially after spending most of your professional life teaching teenagers.

For a start, toilets don't answer back. Regardless of the state their occupiers left them in (and on the whole, most guests were impeccably clean), the toilet quietly accepted whatever you were about to do to it. No remonstrations. No back-chat. Also, like students, some toilets are clean and very rarely give cause for concern whilst some are horrendous. The same brush deals with both loos albeit with a little more elbow grease on the latter sort.

It was also lovely not having to spend hours planning and preparing the night before, explaining to yourself just how you were going to clean the toilet. No writing down the objectives, no explaining what methodology you were going to use, no groupings necessary; it didn't matter if you cleaned the toilets in groups or individually and there was no desired outcomes section to fill in (this one is pretty obvious – a clean loo with no shit on the side!).

There is also the intrinsic satisfaction of seeing a gleaming, white, shining toilet in front of you and knowing that at least if nothing else would go to plan that day, you had made a good job of that particular toilet. Quite a sense of achievement!

Jo, on the other hand, had a much more pragmatic and focussed attitude to cleaning toilets. Her job was to check the toilets after I'd cleaned them and stamp her seal of approval on the loo in the form of a "Sanitised for your protection" ribbon.

There was no getting away from it: toilets were very important. One customer in particular was a delightful gentleman married to an overbearing, ambitious business woman with a penchant for pin stripe suits. She was woman with a mission. The only mission her poor husband had however was to get to a toilet at every possible opportunity.

'Don't be silly, Sidney,' she'd say to her husband, 'you've just been.'

I saw the helpless look in his eyes as he requested a key to the toilet, and I gave it to him regardless of what his wife said.

As the poor man carried her heavy suitcases up and down the stairs, beads of perspiration were running down his cheek. He sat down to catch his breath only to look at me and say pleadingly, 'You don't think I can possibly use your toilet do you?'

Perhaps the very worst incident involving bathrooms was the accident in the room above our private living area in the guest house. It involved two lads who were over for a lads' night out. First impressions are often very accurate ones, but in this case I hold my hands up and say I got it completely wrong.

The two quite large blokes had booked a twin room for the night. They made no pretence about the fact that they were here to have a "bloody good time". We automatically knew this would involve quite a lot of drinking and hoped it would stay there.

'What time would you two lads like breakfast?'

'As late as possible!' came the reply.

I informed them that we served up until half past nine, but if it was a bit later than that, it wouldn't matter as we prided ourselves on our flexibility – something the larger hotels couldn't compete with.

As we were full that particular Saturday night, breakfast was busy. Jo had to clean a few tables to accommodate everyone and so the time flew by very quickly. Before long, it was 9 o'clock and there was no sign of "the lads". She decided to give them until the last customers finished, then clear the dining room and that would be that.

All of a sudden, Jo let out a huge scream and pointed to the ceiling in our private area.

Water was cascading from the gap in between the ceiling and the coving, obviously coming from the en-suite in the room upstairs. And, of course, this just happened to be the room where "the lads" were staying.

Seeing red, I charged up to the room and without knocking, opened the door with the master key to find one of the lads drying his large torso with a bath sheet that appeared to be totally ill-equipped for the job.

'What the hell are you doing?' I demanded to know.

'Had a shower and drying myself mate,' calmly replied one half of the double act.

The other was still hidden below the duvet snoring away, oblivious to the Fawlty-esque exchange taking place right next to him.

'What the hell have you been doing in the shower?' I demanded to know, and charged into an otherwise quiet and undisturbed en-suite.

I blurted how water had been pouring through the ceiling below and asked if his friend would give the shower a miss until I'd got to the bottom of what was causing the leak.

'No worries, mate,' replied the guest and continued drying himself and spraying deodorant everywhere.

The leaking had stopped by now and luckily, the damage had been small. I was muttering to myself something about the lads who'd been stomping about in the shower knocking into everything in a blurry eyed state. Even as I was thinking this, the lads came downstairs and apologised for whatever they were supposed to have done and even asked for a card as they were planning on returning later on in the year!

Before long, we were all shipshape again and the plumber informed us he would be there within a couple of days. Luckily, the room was empty until the following Wednesday, so there was plenty of time to sort things out.

When Dan arrived to assess the job, there was no panicking, which was the hallmark of my plumbing exploits! Instead, he approached things in a cold and logical way, trying to work out what could have been the cause of the leak.

He checked the seals around the shower and was confident that that wasn't the problem. He then told me he'd check the connection under the water tray and asked me to go outside to see if he could see any movement coming from the waste pipe.

'See anything?' he shouted.

'Yes, the whole pipe's coming out of the side of the building!'

'That's your problem!' he said. 'It's come completely out of the connection. Wonder how the hell that happened?'

All of a sudden, I went very quiet.

'You OK, Mike?' shouted Danny from the upstairs window.

'Yes, OK,' I replied. 'I think I know how the pipe was pulled out of the connection!'

I went up to the twin room where Danny was lying under the shower reconnecting the drainage pipe. It was like a confessor going to church on a Saturday evening to cleanse himself of his sins.

'Father, forgive me, for I have sinned. Sorry, Danny, it was me. I did it!'

Danny rolled around in laughter as I recalled the story of the two large lads rolling about the room that Sunday morning. He laughed even more when I told him how I had tried to tackle the out of control ivy growing up the side of the building and how one particular stubborn clump growing around the waste pipe was very reluctant to come away from wall.

'I had to really tug at it and I think I might have just pulled the pipe out a little bit, but I did push it back in again as far it would go!'

'There you are then,' said Danny, 'problem solved!'

Now confessing your sins is one thing. But, penance is another. In this case, three Hail Marys and an Our Father seemed inappropriate.

I, therefore, phoned the lad who had booked and explained to him just how the leak occurred and offered them a night as our guests when (or rather, if) they chose to return.

Confessing does wonders for your conscience!

According to Holland House records, the lads have yet to return and take up their offer of a complimentary night at the guest house. I wonder why?

Chapter 8
The Hotel Inspector Calls

Whenever I think of a hotel inspector, I invariably think of Bernard Cribbins as the demanding spoon salesman, Mr Hutchinson, in the fourth episode of *Fawlty Towers*. Basil Fawlty wrongly suspects he is the inspector and can't do enough to make his stay as pleasant as possible, including physically dragging guests from window tables in the dining room and apologising profusely for the fact that the peas in the omelette are frozen as opposed to fresh. If you remember, Mr Hutchinson declines the omelette and orders a cheese salad instead, insisting peas are a most integral part of the omelette.

Once the confusion has been revealed, Basil is all too eager to unleash his venom on the hapless salesman, and one of the classic scenes is of him and Manuel throwing custard pies in Mr Hutchinson's face as he leaves the hotel – only to reveal the shock at the very end of that episode when a grinning, self-satisfied Fawlty looks up at three suited business men – probably the real hotel inspectors!

Our first dealing with the hotel inspector thankfully did not involve custard pies or peas – either frozen or fresh. In fact, we did not even realise that the hotel inspector was staying with us.

For those unfamiliar with the role of the inspector (probably the majority of people reading this), they are employed (or at least the ones visiting us were) by the Tourist Agency, VisitBritain. They are the organisation who award the star rating displayed on many hotels and guest houses. At the time, we were registered as a four star establishment with VisitBritain, and of course had all the signs and stickers proudly on display to confirm this.

The inspector had checked in anonymously under a non de guerre or assumed name. I think it was Mr Atkinson.

That breakfast had been fairly uneventful with a mixture of guests staying for leisure and business purposes – the latter of course, including Mr "Atkinson".

It was only when he was ready to check out after I presented the bill and processed the payment did he pass me his business card.

I took the card and at first wasn't sure what to do with it. Had he given it to me as a keepsake or was he expecting I did something with it? Display it in a prominent position in case any guest staying just happened to need whatever it was Mr Atkinson was selling or providing. Spoons didn't even cross my mind at this point. He suggested that I might want to look at the card in more detail.

I examined the card carefully and the first clue was a VisitEngland red rose logo printed clearly at the top next to the main heading "Quality in Tourism". I nodded to myself, impressed at the credentials of the guest and his obviously important strategic role in the tourism industry and it was only then that the penny dropped.

No, please tell me this is not happening to me! I thought and looked up and smiled at the "guest" who was not a legitimate guest at all but a hotel inspector!

'Yes, thank you,' replied Mr Knight (not Mr Atkinson!) and suggested we sit down somewhere so we could discuss his findings.

'Perhaps you'd like to ask your wife to join us, if she's free?'

I escorted the inspector to the half-cleared dining room, offered him a tea or coffee and ran through to the back where Jo was quietly washing up listening to the Jack Johnson CD we had put on during breakfast. We often put this particular CD on when we had no real grasp of the sort of people staying with us. Sometimes the Classic FM is the obvious choice, and we clearly avoided hits from the '60s and '70s if anyone was going to a funeral. The difficult one was the Gilbert and Sullivan convention in the summer. We have no Gilbert and Sullivan CDs and think maybe they get to listen to enough light opera during the course of the day to be subjected to *Behold the Lord High Executioner* as they take off the top of their lightly boiled eggs.

Jo wondered why I had taken so long to finish up.

'Your coffee's here. Shall we sit down or…'

'Before you go any further, you need to come with me to the dining room and meet someone!'

Jo smiled when she saw the gentleman seated at one of the tables. She noticed that he had his laptop open and a large file next to it.

Her initial thoughts were that he was here to try to sell them something and so she began to prepare herself for a gruelling sales pitch – something that she did not relish after a full service and six rooms waiting to be stripped and made ready for a group of Swiss botanists due to arrive later that day.

'Jo, please meet Mr Knight, the HOTEL INSPECTOR.'

Her initial response was one of relief. At least she was not in for a long-winded sales talk and hours of do we or don't we agonising.

We sat down with the Quality Assessor for half an hour or so before escorting him on a guided tour of the house. He insisted on going into each room to scrutinise the quality of the bedding, the en-suite facilities and general decor.

I tried to make light of the "inspection". Each time we opened a room, I insisted on going into the en-suite to make sure no unpleasant surprises were lurking anywhere!

When he had completed his tour, we returned to the dining room where the inspector picked up his large file and made a few scribbles on a note pad before ticking a few boxes on the questionnaire. He put his pen down and handed a small card to me.

'Congratulations,' he said, 'you've retained your four star rating!'

My wife and I beamed at each other. Though we took over the running of Holland House as a Four Star establishment, we soon learnt that the stars were awarded not to the property but to the proprietors. Now our four stars were legitimate!

However, before we got down to any serious high fiving and celebrating, he was keen to add that we shouldn't get too carried away and that there was still a lot of room for improvement.

Our respective grins temporarily vanished as we adopted the serious corporate frown expression, though inwardly yelling to ourselves, *Get in there!*

Mr Knight pointed out that the door handle inside the room he'd been staying in needed replacing, and he also referred to the large French dresser in the dining room. We had been fairly recently informed by an antique dealer staying with us that it would have been made in Austria in the mid-eighteenth century for export to the United States. It was very much a focal point for discussion among guests, and in those awkward moments when no one knew what to say, it was a point of conversation.

'That's a wonderful piece of furniture!' they would say. 'Did you bring it with you when you moved here?'

Apart from the aesthetic quality of the large piece of furniture, it was also very practical. We set out all the cereals, milk and fruit juices on it as well as storing a myriad of breakfast "stuff" inside, so when the inspector mooted the idea of selling it, we were rather stunned.

'Mm, will have to think about that one...' hoping my response was enough to satisfy the Inspector and send him on his way, knowing we would not be troubled by any incognito "Quality Assessors" for a couple of years.

Evidently, the secret guest made an appearance only on alternative years, and the year in between, a scheduled visit was arranged.

I thanked the inspector and escorted him to the front door, waited a few minutes while his car drove out of the car park before daring to let out a loud yell, which must have been heard all over Harrogate.

The feeling was very similar to a post-Ofsted inspection – particularly when the results had been positive. Kids would be asked to get on with something quiet and not too taxing – a DVD was often a good place to start while teachers walked on a cloud all day and planned which pub they'd meet at after school to celebrate properly. We had no desire to carry on cleaning rooms and would have quite happily gone out into town for a drink or two!

One of the difficulties I have noticed since giving up teaching was not having my year punctuated with things like holidays and exams to help me gauge the passing of time. Now, working for ourselves, we had to use other mileposts, and often could be heard expressing amazement that a whole year had passed by since the last Great Yorkshire Show, Knitting and Stitching Conference or repeat visitors returning for an annual break in the Yorkshire Spa town.

June 2008

We similarly had a "surely it can't be a whole year since" reaction when VisitEngland contacted us to book an appointment for their Quality Assessor, Mr Knight, to visit us.

'Isn't that the same guy who came last year?' asked Jo.

This time we were quite prepared for the meeting when Mr Knight arrived. We embarked upon the guided tour and were looking forward to dazzling the inspector with a couple of shiny new en-suite bathrooms as well as some freshly decorated rooms – minus flowers and swirls! I made sure I held on tight to the door handle in one room that we hadn't got round to changing since his last surprise visit, but I wondered if Mr Knight had in fact read the same script as they had. He appeared not too bothered at all by the updated facilities (or the missing door handle), but was more concerned with the aesthetic value of the art we had on display in the rooms.

'Now take this wall for example,' Mr Knight pointed out. 'You have only one painting here and it's screaming for another to balance it out. And yet here, there are too many paintings – it is far too busy. You need to simplify what's on this wall to make a more relaxing atmosphere for guests.'

We nodded in appreciation, though secretly wondered why the hell we were paying several hundreds of pounds to VisitBritain when the only advice we were been given was where to hang a print of Malham Cove!

When we had completed the art appreciation tour, we returned to the dining room. I was keen to point out as quickly as I could that whilst they appreciated the inspector's advice on what to do with the large dresser, we had in fact decided to hold on to it – though Mr Knight got in there before either of us could say could anything.

'That's a lovely piece of furniture, isn't it? It really goes well in the room and makes a wonderful focal point.'

Jo looked at me in disbelief.

'Yes, we appreciated your advice the last time you came, but we decided to hold on to it.'

'What advice was that?' queried Mr Knight.

'To take it to the furniture auctions…'

'No. That wouldn't have been me. I would never give out advice like that!'

'Yes, you did, Mr Knight,' I pointed out.

'No. No. Definitely not me; must have been someone else.'

I looked at Jo and we instantaneously knew that now was the time to drop this issue; to let go while the going was still promising.

'It must have been someone else. Strange!'

With that, the inspector scribbled something on a form and ticked a few boxes before handing over the only thing that did matter: not paintings or dressers, but the confirmation of our retaining the four stars!

One Great Yorkshire Show, Christmas, end of the financial year and Eurovision Song Contest later, thoughts once again returned to the idea of the mystery guest.

At the time, we were still very enthusiastic about running the guest house, and religiously kept an eye open for single people staying during the week. We'd let each other know if we spotted any suspicious bookings that just might be an incognito inspector armed with a book on art appreciation and Victorian handles.

I nearly told Jo to "flag up any suspicions", but thankfully resisted using consultancy-speak in my own guesthouse – one of the main reasons I left the teaching profession in the first place.

Weeks and months passed without any contender for the Hotel Inspector showing up and by this point, we'd almost become immune from any fear from one calling.

June 2009

We had a good social life in Harrogate and one particular evening, arranged to meet some of our friends at a pub in town. We were only waiting for one guest (yes I know, we should have known!) who said he'd arrive at 6:30 as he'd been travelling from Leicester (you've got it reader, haven't you).

I checked the reservations diary and the missing guest was one Mr Cox. Once he was in, we could hit the town. Pete and Phil would be there by now, and I do enjoy that relaxing pint before heading into the restaurant for the formal sitting down bit.

I decided I'd give him a ring as he may have been held up by traffic and might not be arriving until much later.

As usual, I complained about not being able to read Jo's handwriting but eventually managed to connect with the given number. This did not bode well as the number was a landline and not a mobile. The chances are that unless Mrs Cox answered the phone (or another Mr Cox for that matter) we would not get a reply as our guest would likely to be following the directions of North on the M1.

The telephone went into answer phone mode.

'Hello. Am I speaking with Mr Cox? Hi Mr Cox, it's Mike here from Holland House. You have a room with us tonight and I'm ringing to find out what time you're likely to be with us this evening?'

The reception was not brilliant. It appeared as if Mr Cox was still driving which meant he could be miles from Harrogate. 'We are going out tonight so the chances are that when you arrive, we'll have gone. I will leave the key to your room hanging on the mirror in the hall; it's Room 1 and the red key opens the front door. Thanks now, Mr Cox,' and with that, I put the phone down and went to get my coat. 'He's still on his way so I've told him I've left the key to his room in the hall. You ready?'

Jo heard me shouting something from upstairs. She knew that I was eager to go, but she didn't want to leave until she was sure everything was ready for breakfast the following morning. She checked that there was enough bacon and that the sausages had been taken out of the deep freeze. She opened the fridge and quickly scanned the contents: milk, fruit and butter.

'Come on, Jo!' I yelled.

'I'm checking we have everything for tomorrow. Someone has to be sensible around here!'

Jo grabbed her coat and bag. We were just about ready to close the front door behind us when I spotted a light in the car park.

'Oh fuck! Just as we're ready to go! It's Mr Cox!'

'What shall we do?'

'Might as well check him in. Still got plenty of time and I'd feel happier knowing he was in and the key wasn't hanging in the hall.'

I peered through to the car park. I saw a tall gentleman emerge from a rather low two-seater sports car and something registered in my visual memory. I looked closely again and I knew that this guest had been here before.

'This Mr Cox. He's been here before; I recognise him.'

With that, Mr Cox made his way round to the front of the house and was walking up the stairs to the front hall. He peered round – obviously looking for a key hanging somewhere in the vicinity of the mirror and I opened the door.

'Welcome!'

'Oh thank you. So very kind of you to wait until I arrived!'

I stared in disbelief. If this was Mr Cox, then I was Florence Nightingale! This was Mr Knight – the Hotel Inspector!

'No problems – welcome. Glad you got here before we went out.'

I handed "Mr Cox" a guest registration form which he dutifully filled in as Mr Cox from an address in Leicester. If this was his way of trying to hide his true identity, then he was not doing a very good job of it. For goodness sake – I'd met him twice, had detailed intensive conversations with him and now he was here a third time, and it was getting totally surreal. I just decided to play along with the charade though I felt it was obvious that the inspector now knew the game was over and his alias had been blown! I was many things, but not a good actor!

The rest of the evening was a blur. We were not able to concentrate. There was no point in even attempting to recall the evening's events to any of our friends! Who in their right mind would believe us? We decided that the best we could do was to rehearse the breakfast scenario in the morning and prepared ourselves for the revelation.

"Mr Cox" turned up for his breakfast at about eight thirty.

I told Jo to brace herself and followed the Hotel Inspector into the dining room. 'Good morning, Mr Cox!' I announced loudly enough for the world to hear.

The Hotel Inspector was too busy perusing the various fresh fruits and yoghurts. He turned round to find me standing behind him with a bemused grin on my face.

'Oh sorry, yes, good morning,' he mumbled unconvincingly.

I realised that now was moment to launch my master plan. It had come to me in the middle of the night and I wondered why I hadn't thought of it sooner than I did. It was the ideal way of wriggling out of the ridiculously embarrassing fact that I knew who Mr Cox really was, and that Mr Knight knew I did!

'Excuse me, but do you mind me asking – have you been on television at all?'

'Oh, I've been accused of many things but acting certainly isn't one of them!' replied Mr Cox.

'Strange! You must have a doppelganger then! We have had quite a few actors staying with us over the past few weeks. Only last month Herr Ulrich aka Peter Birch stayed with us. He starred in the first episode of Auf Wiedersehen Pet. I think there's some sort of arts convention happening somewhere so I just assumed you were here for that as well.'

Jo took Mr Knight (or was it Mr Cox?) his breakfast and then sat back and waited for the inevitable to happen, and it did – just as we'd anticipated.

'Thanks for a very enjoyable stay, and here's my business card.'

We did not have to look at the card to know what it was. I simply looked hard at it, planning what my reaction was going to be.

'I knew I recognised you from somewhere!' I exclaimed, 'I was sure I knew you from the TV but of course now I know why!'

'I really thought I'd blown my cover when I arrived yesterday. I was sure you recognised me instantly!'

'Not at all,' Jo lied through her teeth. 'We thought we recognised you, but as Mike said, we were sure it was from the telly!'

Formalities were dispensed with and the statutory four stars awarded.

We thanked Mr Knight (we could use his real name now) and wished him a pleasant onward journey.

'I hope you don't come again as our secret guest!' I added. 'Not that we have anything against you, but I think that we might recognise you next time.'

Must do something about that door handle in Room 1.

Chapter 9
The Great Yorkshire Show

'Full English; bacon medium to well done, please.'

'Thank you. Would you like brown or white toast?'

'Wholemeal.'

I returned to the kitchen. 'Who does that pretentious twat think he is? Bacon medium to well done!'

'Is that what he said?' exclaimed Jo with a huge smirk on her face. 'He obviously thinks he's in one of the posh restaurants he goes to in Knightsbridge; did you offer to show him the drinks menu?'

'He'd probably ask if the orange juice was freshly squeezed this morning.'

I returned to the dining room and already a new guest had sat down next to "Michael Winner". They were all wine merchants – up from London for the Great Yorkshire Show. Although the show was traditionally an agricultural show – the largest one in the country to be exact – visitors could buy anything they wanted there from a holiday home in France to a new Land Rover; a winter coat to an outdoor Jacuzzi or a hot tub. Gone are the days when it was just an agricultural show. They still have the sheep shearing, livestock displays, show jumping and that sort of thing, but many people go there primarily to sample the vast array of food and drink on offer – including fine wines from SW11.

The majority of the people staying for this particular years' show (and most years for that fact) were either exhibitors or livestock judges. Visitors tended to just come up for the day, and very few actually stayed overnight – not there would be much availability if they wanted to. This year we had a Berkshire pig judge; two directors of an agricultural machinery company; a family of Guinea pig breeders; a couple of regular visitors who produced local honey and of course, the wine merchants from SW11!

They had annoyed me the moment they arrived.

In fact, several sets of guests had caused one problem or another when arriving with their vehicles at different stages during the day.

The wine merchants turned up in two huge Land Rovers, taking up half of the car park. I wanted to make some snide comment, but thought the better of it. I didn't want them to think I was a hard done by Northerner with a chip on my shoulder as well. Sometimes I forgot I was a guest house proprietor, and wore my left wing hat with a legitimate axe to grind about the inequalities and unfairness of life in Britain too often at times for Jo's liking.

Now my job was to host posh people in Harrogate.

I had turned my back on the teaching profession to run a business for people regardless of their class, political or sexual persuasion and that included Wine Merchants from London.

'We have three rooms booked for the next three nights under the name Smythe.'

I winced when I heard that. Whatever modern Sociologists thought, names like this perpetuated the class system in this country. I thought that perhaps a double barrelled name would be more appropriate – something like Ponsonby-Smythe maybe? Whatever the guest's name, whether it was Smythe or Smith, I had to remember that MY role was to make these people feel welcomed and not take the piss out of them: at the end of the day, their money was just as good as anyone else's!

I was actually in the car park when they had arrived. Normally, I would have offered to bring them in through the tradesman's entrance (back door to be exact!). Guests usually had to avoid bumping into bags of soiled laundry. Quite often, if someone had mobility issues, particularly elderly customers, they were grateful for being able to access the house through the rear entrance thereby avoiding the steep steps at the front.

This lot can make their own way round to the main entrance though.

I welcomed them to Harrogate and the Great Yorkshire Show.

Unlike the wine merchants, when the directors of the agricultural machinery company arrived, they rang the front door bell. I opened it and two burly, well-set gentlemen walked in.

'WE HAVE A RESERVATION HERE FOR THREE NIGHTS,' screamed one of the blokes. 'THE NAME'S PRESTON, DAVE PRESTON.'

Why did he have to shout? The noise level physically hurt my ears. I got the guests to complete all the necessary paperwork and informed them where breakfast would be served in the morning.

'CAN YOU TELL ME WHERE THE CAR PARK IS? WE HAVE A VEHICLE WE NEED TO PARK UP BEFORE WE GO TO THE SHOW.'

I took them to the front of the house and saw a massive fire engine, red, four-wheel drive truck parked on the opposite side of the road.

'Oh shit!'

The tyres were twice the height and thickness size of normal ones and it appeared to have every gadget and appendage in the book, and gave a middle finger to every tree hugger and paid up member of the Green Party in the country.

'Is that your vehicle?'

'YES.'

This was going to be a problem. The wine merchants already had two large four wheel drives in the car park and now this brute!

'Will you need the vehicle to get to the show?'

'NO, ONCE IT'S HERE, WE'LL LEAVE IT UNTIL WE CHECK OUT ON THURSDAY MORNING.'

I arranged it so that these blokes could park their monster next to the house and persuaded the wine merchants to move their vehicles, which seemed quite modest in comparison. Once this big boy was in the car park, nothing would get past it, and the wine merchants needed their vehicles every day to re-stock their tent.

After serving Michael Winner his Full English with bacon medium to well-done, I asked if anyone wanted anything else. I enjoyed getting into the dining room and meeting people – something I was not able to do when we were really busy.

'Are you guys finished here?'

'THANK YOU VERY MUCH. WE'RE OFF T'SHOW NOW.'

'Hope you have a good show; see you later on.'

I collected their dirty plates and cutlery; I still could not understand why they shouted all the time – perhaps it was because they were always talking around loud vehicles?

I then went over to the family of three sitting in the window table. Jo was right, I thought. The area stank and my mind wandered back to Peter and Mary who had rewarded us with two weeks of their smelly antics earlier on in the year.

The small animal breeders had travelled all the way from mid Wales in a small vehicle with luggage in the boot and the guinea pigs in a cage on the back seat. They had telephoned Holland House to inform us of their expected arrival time and to let us know that the father had serious mobility issues.

'Come in via the rear entrance,' I informed them, 'no point having to trail right around the front late at night.'

When the lights of their car were eventually spotted turning into the car park, I rushed out and got them to park up next to the garage. Once they had come to a complete standstill, I opened a door and welcomed them to Harrogate.

Now I have a great deal of difficulty in even beginning to explain the smell that hit me when the door had been opened. It was a mixture of stale BO, animals, straw and manure – though not necessarily in that order.

I was not sure where the smell of manure came from. They told me they lived on a smallholding, but they didn't bring that with them did they? Or possibly they did!

I helped them with their suitcases and noticed when I returned downstairs, they had left a trail of straw and dried mud behind them on our red carpet. I picked up the largest bits by hand, but there was no way I could use a vacuum cleaner at this time of night; it would have to wait until the morning.

'Did you cook that splendid breakfast, Mike?' questioned a portly, fresh-faced Irishman sitting on his own. 'I always say you can judge a hotel on the quality of its bacon and that was fine meat, sir!'

'Very kind of you,' I replied, shaking the gentleman's hand and welcoming him to Holland House. 'Are you here for the show as well?'

'That I am,' and the gentleman produced a business card from his top pocket and handed it over: Vaughan Byrne. Breeder and Judge of Prize Berkshire pigs.

Mr Byrne was not only a pig breeder but a raconteur extraordinaire, because at ten thirty, when both of us should have been hard at it servicing the rooms, we found ourselves sitting down at one of our own tables, together with the honey producers and the guinea pig breeders listening to, and enthralled by, the tales and exploits of a pig breeder.

In less than an hour, he had covered topics ranging from the making of a Channel Four drama production, Blandings, involving a prize pig (Vaughan's role being to help Timothy Spall bring the best out of the reluctant four footed thespian) to pig husbandry and how intelligent the Berkshire was in particular. He was proud of the fact that his own prize pigs descended directly from the most sought after boar bloodlines – Peter Lad and Freight Train.

Just as we thought he had finished, he went on to explain how Jamie Oliver was a huge supporter of the Berkshire breed, and he described the alcohol-fuelled nights he and Jamie had shared travelling around the Emerald Isle in search of local ingredients for the celebrity chef's latest TV series.

I looked at my watch and reluctantly pointed out that we would really have to get cracking otherwise nothing would get done. Luckily, most of the guests were staying over so none of the rooms required a complete change over.

Sod the time though, I thought. We came into the business to meet interesting characters like that; it's a pity there aren't more about like him!

Jo agreed. She found these characters fascinating; a flash back to times past when conversation was alive and people simply talked to each other. She liked the Irish people for that – although at times struggled to understand everything they said.

I remember one Irish guest who was much less communicative than the majority of his fellow nationals, however. When I asked him what he would like for breakfast, his reply was 'sausages'.

Unsure I had heard him correctly, I repeated the question and again, got the reply, 'sausages!'

We were unsure what to do. I remember thinking, you can't give the guy just a sausage, and in the end we decided to give him two sausages on a plate together with a rack of toast.

He devoured them, and the next day he ordered 'sausages' again, but this time with much more gusto and enthusiasm. We both agreed this warranted three sausages.

By the end of his four-day stay, we had increased his portion to four sausages and he was a happy customer.

When he came to pay, he put the card in the machine but told us he didn't know his pin number. We were surprised that after three attempts, the payment went through, but the card machine requested a customer signature.

This also caused some confusion and the poor fellow turned round to go back to his room. He told us he was going to get his passport to remind himself how he signed his name!

Jo always hoped I would answer the telephone if anyone from Ireland or Scotland rang. Although she managed to get the dates and card details right, she often struggled understanding the email addresses. Since taking over the running of the guest house, we are both completely familiar with the phonetic alphabet – a result of having had too many confirmation emails returned to us with an invalid address message.

I was dreading going into Room 8 – the guinea pig breeders!

We made our way upstairs to their room on the top floor. Any detective would have had no difficulty working out which room they had been staying in; the trail of straw and dried mud gave it away immediately. I gingerly opened the door to their room.

'Oh déjà-fucking-vu!' I screeched!

'Is it bad?'

'Bad! The English language has no words to describe what it smells like in here,' I protested, peering into the "Black Hole of Calcutta".

The curtains were drawn and all the electric heaters were on full blast. I drew back the curtains and opened the windows to feel a blast of clean fresh air hitting me on the face. The bedding was everywhere and I struggled to comprehend how people could leave a room in such a state. What puzzled me more was the straw scattered everywhere – even in the beds!

'Surely not…'

I felt a cold shudder run through my body and told myself not to think such thoughts. I attacked the room; I felt I should have been wearing wellington boots and overalls. The sheets, even after one night, needed changing, and then we vacuumed the rest of the room.

'How the hell do we get rid of this smell?'

I picked up a pillow and sniffed it before throwing it down in disgust, 'Ugh! Christ Almighty, smell that!'

'I'd rather not. I'll take your word for it. This lot will go straight in the wash when they leave the day after tomorrow.'

'Look! There's even straw in the shower!'

'Have they had those bloody animals up here?'

I ran downstairs, but their car had already gone. I'd brought them up to their room the previous night – even carried a heavy suitcase for them – but I was sure the cage had remained in their car.

We used a spray air freshener – something we generally tried to avoid – but in such extreme cases environmental concerns were not the first priority, and the room was filled with hints of fresh linen and CFC's.

'God I hope we have no environmentalists staying with us as well, what with all this air freshener and that massive gas guzzling monster parked up at the back!'

Yet another one for the memoirs, I thought, as I locked the door to their room behind me, shaking my head in disbelief.

Between us we could finish the rooms fairly quickly when no one was checking out, but because we had to completely "muck one out", it had taken us quite a bit of time. We had been given some free entry tickets to the show by the lovely bee keeping couple, but by the time we finished, all I just wanted was to sit down and relax in front of the TV and watch *Homes under the Hammer.*

I remembered one very bemusing conversation with Steve, a fellow Guest House proprietor during a Coffee Morning. He was discussing the morning ritual after breakfasts:

'We always get the dining room cleaned first before we tackle any of the bedrooms,' said Steve, 'then we make a start on the rooms – but we always make sure we have a break when Homes Under the Hammer is on.'

Every time I saw *Homes under the Hammer*, I thought about Steve and his wife sitting down taking a break.

'Thank goodness we haven't reached that stage yet!'

The rest of the afternoon and evening passed without incident. We decided we'd ask the honey producers if we could buy some jars (if they had any left). We'd been given some the previous year and it was absolutely delicious. It was only just before I was contemplating going to bed, that one of our guests knocked on the door to our private living room.

'Excuse me, but I have a request.'

I jumped up to find one of the Wine Merchants from SW11 standing in the doorway holding a box.

'Sorry, can I help you?'

'The director of our company sent these tea towels over late this afternoon. He wants them washed and ready for tomorrow. Prince Charles is due at the show tomorrow and he wants everything to be just right! Do you think you could put these in the washing machine for us and have them ready for tomorrow morning?'

I looked at Jo.

I could tell by the expression on her face that the polite answer to his question would be go stick them where the sun does not shine!

We looked at each other.

'I'd be very, very, grateful; you'd be doing us a huge favour!'

I decided I'd take the initiative and agree to his request. I knew Jo would be pissed off with me, but I'd put that right. I would personally do all the work.

'Go on then; pass them over.'

I dared not look at Jo, but waited until the guest had returned upstairs before she launched the anticipated attack.

'Why the hell did you agree to do that for those arrogant snobs?'

'Listen – it won't take much effort; I'll do all the work, but I bet there's got to be a few bottles – maybe even a crate – in this for us.'

'Do you really think so?'

'Course! They can't let something like this go unrewarded! This was a request from their director so they'll be delighted that we've agreed to do it for them! I'll put 'em in the machine now and hang 'em up when they're ready. Then, when I wake up, I'll put them all in the tumble dryer and then it's just a matter of folding them up and putting them back in the box. Easy!'

Jo was still shaking her head unconvinced while I ran downstairs to the laundry room and shoved them in on a quick thirty degree wash.

Although I was quite tired, I waited until the wash was completed before hanging the thirty or so teacloths up in the laundry room.

When the wine merchants arrived in the dining room the next morning, I proudly handed over a box full of clean fresh tea towels!

'Thank you,' muttered Mr Smythe, turning immediately to his colleague saying 'Right, I want you to make sure that all the wines are on display and that no samples are given out before the Royal visit.'

I stood there like a first year pupil wanting for praise from his teacher, but realised none would be forthcoming. Not even a well done lad and a patronising pat on the head.

'What can I get you for the cooked breakfasts?'

'Three Full English,' said one of the colleagues looking at the other two nodding in agreement.

'Bacon medium to well done for me,' echoed the third guest dressed in an open check shirt complete with bright blue cravat.

I fucking hate cravats!

Chapter 10
That 3-Letter Word: S-E-X

After running the guest house for a few months or so, I found myself chatting casually to Dave, the proprietor at a neighbouring guesthouse.

'One bit of advice I'll give you for nothing – never accept a booking for two single women in a twin room on a Saturday night!'

I wished Dave had passed that piece of advice a few weeks earlier. However, even if he had, it seemed a rather dangerous and a highly politically incorrect thing to discriminate against single ladies sharing a twin room on a night out. Hundreds of ladies sharing a twin room had passed through Holland House without incident and so this one-off perhaps should just be put down to experience.

Jo had taken the booking by telephone and commented on how pleasant the lady sounded. At least she seemed to remember thinking the lady sounded nice; it was several weeks before arriving that they had made the booking.

I had gone to the Cash and Carry when they arrived, so Jo welcomed them and checked them in. She got them to sign a guest registration form. She always insisted on this and would get annoyed with me when I didn't follow strict protocol.

I often wondered whose protocol it was? The hotel inspector told us to do it, but then again, he told us to go and sell our prize French dresser then denied even saying this, so I don't know how much credence we could give to Mr Knight. My argument was that as long as we had their names and addresses on the computer system (which we had), then I was not going to create more work, destroy more trees or help the state's obsession with monitoring any more than necessary.

She escorted the guests to their second floor room and wished them a pleasant evening in Harrogate. They told her that they were going to the spa for a pampering session before going out for a meal and a few drinks.

When I asked Jo what they were like, her reply was pretty succinct:

'Tarty!'

The ladies took themselves off for a spa treatment before hitting the town, and naturally we thought that would be the last time we saw them until breakfast.

How wrong could we be.

At about 1.30 in the morning, Jo dug her elbow into my ribs and said, 'Listen! Someone is climbing the fire escape.'

I slowly came out of a post-Match of the Day Saturday night coma and strained to listen. All was in darkness, but I distinctly heard one male voice saying 'Which room did they say they were in?'

'What are you going to do about it?' She asked, sitting bolt upright with a 'you wanted a Guest House so you go and do something about it' attitude.

I think I replied that I didn't know what I was going to do about it – I don't recall any chapters in the "Run Your Own Guest House" book on these sorts of problems. There was plenty of advice on creating welcoming rooms, local advertising and breakfast menus – but nothing on nocturnal intruders.

At this point my wife put on her dressing gown and literally charged upstairs to their room and began to knock assertively on the door. Eventually a face appeared – but it was obvious that we were only going to see a face. Lord knows what else had been going on in the room, but I bet they weren't having a game of Snakes and Ladders.

'No extra visitors are allowed,' said my wife. 'Are you aware of the rule?'

The woman mumbled something about OK and that she would ask the man to leave.

By this time I had emerged and was charging upstairs to provide support and logistical back up. In fact, the only thing I could think of doing was to put the kettle on and make a cup of tea. We sat with a cuppa in front of the CCTV and waited for an appearance of our (or should I say our guest's) visitor.

After a while, we saw someone creeping down the stairs and so we darted to intercept him with a barrage of questions I had been rehearsing for the past 20 minutes or so.

'Do you realise that you are contravening fire regulations?' was the best one I could come up with. I was particularly proud of that one! He couldn't object to or argue with that. Yes, keep it objective and to the point and don't get sucked in by any moralistic high ground sort of stuff.

The visitor wasn't in any way embarrassed or perturbed by the reception awaiting him when he came down the stairs.

'Listen mate,' he replied, 'this bird asked me to her room, and if you'd have been in my shoes, you'd have done exactly the same thing!'

Conscious of my wife standing behind me, I replied in a Basil Fawlty-esque, we are not amused, stiff upper lip and paid up member of the Conservative party tone, 'I most certainly would not!'

At this point the doorbell rang.

What the hell is going on now, I thought! I opened the door only to find our other female guest with a male friend, both eager to run upstairs to the room to have their "turn"!

I wanted to curl up in a ball and the world to swallow me up. I took a deep breath. I wondered what Basil Fawlty would have done, but decided that might not be such a good idea. I did consider forcing them all to leave, but decided that this was probably not the most advisable thing to do. They outnumbered us and I didn't want to get into some sort of squabble in the early hours of the morning. In a flash of inspiration, I advised the "group" that they would all be allowed to go up to the room, but that I insisted on taking payment first.

The male guest who had just eagerly arrived handed me his credit card, which I took payment for the room – twice over!

After all, it was dual occupancy x2, wasn't it?

The guest, although quite drunk, noticed that a fairly hefty chunk had been taken off his credit card. I reassured him and told him that he didn't have to pay for it all: he could take money from the other three occupants.

I smiled and turned round to go back to my own bed and in a soft but none the less discernible tone uttered the words: 'Right my friend, who's been screwed now?'

Even Jo managed a smile as well; what started off as a fairly worrying situation eventually made us giggle at half past two in the morning.

Well, this is the chapter I have been dreading the most. I originally thought of all the incidents, happenings and curious tales we have to relay, the majority would be on the delicate subject of sex. In fact, whenever we met up with our friends, they would always ask if I've got any interesting stories to relate and one of them even used to wink when asking it!

The previous story was our first and to be fair, worst experience regarding nocturnal comings and goings. The fact that it happened only shortly after taking over the running guest house probably set the warning bells chiming unnecessarily – suggesting that we could expect a lot more of this sort of thing. Perhaps they have happened – only we are now too tired to notice!

However, I made my mate roll about with laughter when I recalled my most embarrassing experience regarding this particular "delicate area".

It took place not long after we had taken over the running of the place. Now women often complain that their husbands don't listen to them. I am not in this category of men though. I always hear what my wife says. For example, one day I heard her mention something about towels and Room 6. Point proven, I hear you say?

Well, perhaps not. On my way to carry out some maintenance in our family room, I saw a pile of towels outside Room 6. I picked up the towels and opened the door. The next fraction of a second will be one of the most vivid and shocking moments of my life. Laying on the bed, completely naked, was the wife. However, it was the man who was the object of my untimely intrusion the most. I am a fan of cartoons, particularly Tom and Jerry. Well, the man appeared to be suspended in mid-air in a way that only Hanna and Barbara could have convincingly portrayed. The whole incident would only have lasted a second or two but when I think of it now, it seemed to have been an eternity. The one thing I noticed was that he had both of his hands covering a strategic part of his anatomy and was yelling in slow motion one word:

'NO!!!!!'

Less than a fraction of a second and I'd shut the door.

Even with the door shut I could only visualise the scene and nothing else. The interesting thing is that upon reflection, the lady seemed quite indifferent to the intrusion. Had she not seen me?

What now, I thought?

Funnily enough, my biggest concern was how I was going to look the couple in the eye should I bump into them that evening or the following morning at breakfast. And with a guest house of only eight rooms, it was highly probable that I would meet them.

I found my wife and immediately recalled my embarrassing experience, thinking she'll either sympathise or make me see the funny side of the experience.

However, the only thing she said to me was

'I told you NOT to go into Room 6 with the towels!'

Obviously I deserved that one, and in fact, I did serve the couple at breakfast and it was completely normal. I'm hoping that neither of them saw me. And even if they did there is nothing sensational about recalling a time when a door opened and a man's face appeared for half a second. Hardly News of The World headlines!

Much to my friend's disappointment, many of the stories involving sex or romance turned out to be highly amusing as opposed to "dirty" or "smutty"!

For example, we received a booking for a single room on Valentine's Day. Obviously, this lady was not going to be enjoying a romantic night with any night time "action". However, we received an e mail from her shortly before she was due to arrive. She said she would be arriving at 3pm and she had booked the room to surprise her boyfriend. We assumed "boyfriend" lived in Harrogate and her being here (she lived in Northampton) was the surprise!

However, when she arrived here with her boyfriend, we soon realised that both were going to get a surprise neither of them had anticipated.

The poor lady thought she had booked a double room and was absolutely devastated when I explained to her the mistake she had made.

'I must admit,' she said, 'I thought it did seem a bit cheap – especially on Valentine's Day!'

I apologised, informing them we had no other room.

She apologised to her boyfriend, saying that she'd just made a slight error when booking online.

I said that on this occasion we'd turn a blind eye to fire regulations and allow the two of them to share a single room.

'Just pretend you're teenagers!' I said.

That made them laugh. I believe they had an enjoyable night out in Harrogate, and at least for breakfast they had a table and two chairs.

Not all guests are as romantically inclined however. Wining and dining as a precursor to a night (or afternoon) of passion is not always necessary – especially when you're only sixteen!

It was about two o'clock in the afternoon when the front door bell rang. A young lad stood there, and in a rather nervous, hesitant voice asked me how much double rooms were.

I told him they were ninety pounds.

Turning round to look at his girlfriend, he pondered slightly and replied, 'And how much would it be for an hour?'

Some guests however, are not at all hesitant or nervous about the real reason for their stay, and one particular gentleman became a regular visitor.

The first time he stayed, he had booked a single room but amazingly, by about four o'clock in the afternoon informed me he had just "happened" to have bumped into an old friend and could he swap the room for a double room.

His "friend" was a rather large lady.

At breakfast, and in front of the lady, he pointed out that it was a very tight squeeze in the room between the bed and the radiator. I agreed and apologised in one sentence.

'Oh no,' was his reply, 'no need to apologise. When I had to squeeze by her it was a most pleasant experience!'

Jo found it all less amusing than I did though. On his return visit several months later she really questioned whether we needed to report his visit to someone, and the fact that I thought it best we just turned a blind eye to what was happening did not meet with her approval.

He booked a double room this time, but when he arrived (once again without blinking an eye) he informed that he had booked a night away for him and his…niece!

Even I found this rather uncomfortable to deal with, especially since he had not booked two single rooms or even a twin room: he'd booked a double! When I broached this fact to him, he shrugged his shoulders as if it were a mere oversight on his part.

'Oh dear, how careless I am, aren't I, dear,' turning to look at his very young "niece". 'Never mind,' he said, 'we'll manage somehow, won't we, dear?'

Now if I were to continue and recall a further visit from this gentleman, but this time bringing with him two young lads, you would think I am really exaggerating and making things up. The short answer is that I am not exaggerating or making things up at all.

However, I think we'll leave it at that now and go back to recalling a story that makes me smile as opposed to one that makes me wince. I would rather a delightful 77-year-old-lady from Alice Springs, a remote town in Australia's Northern Territory have the last word in this particular "delicate" section.

She had been born in Harrogate but emigrated when she was a young girl. She eventually met and married an Aboriginal gentleman and went on to have a family. She was over on a nostalgia trip and told us that it was most certainly the last trip she would make so all in all it was an emotional time for her.

What's this to do with sex I hear the reader saying?

She had planned on the Sunday to visit Harewood House. For those unaware, Harewood House is the ancestral home of Lord Harewood, the Queen's cousin. It's situated half way between Harrogate and Leeds. To help her, I checked on the internet and was sorry to disappoint the lady and tell her that it was closed and wouldn't be open until the spring.

On the Monday morning for breakfast, the dining room was quite full. Most of the guests were over for a quiet break. We had our Classic FM CD playing in the background and the atmosphere was very relaxed.

Our Australian guest came down, and after she ordered breakfast, I asked her what she had done the previous day. She said she'd been to a new Everyman Cinema which had just recently opened.

I asked her what she'd been to see and quite openly and clearly she announced for all in the dining room to hear, 'Fifty Shades Darker!'

Everyone, including me, erupted into spontaneous laughter – even the lady herself.

'I hadn't heard of it and I thought it would be a horror film!' she added. 'However, it was throwing it down with rain outside and I didn't know what to do, so I just stayed on until the end.'

'Well, that's your side of the story!' I said, winking at her and exchanging smiles with the other customers before trotting off to get her breakfast.

Chapter 11
Trip Advisor and Other "Problems"

'Good morning. Andy Bingham's the name: senior reviewer with trip advisor.'

I didn't know what to make of this pompous guest as he strolled into the entrance hall holding a clipboard and pencil in one hand, and removing his half-moon spectacles from his face with the other! Was I supposed to be impressed? A little intimidated?

He put his "business card" on the table (yes he'd had one made – complete with an owl logo!) After brief introductions, it transpired our latest guest was an ex-chemistry teacher: this might explain why he pretended to be an Ofsted inspector. After just a few verbal exchanges, it became perfectly obvious he had been a very bad teacher; probably bullied mercilessly by the kids and chased out by senior management – bribed with an early pension deal he couldn't afford to reject. He now had the power and status he had clearly sought to achieve during his working life; he was finally somebody!

Mr Bingham stayed with us for two days and obviously wrote the statutory review: we were awarded a satisfactory. In the comment, he pointed out that it would have been good, but the water pressure in our top room was too low to warrant anything above a satisfactory.

Twat.

Like it or loathe it, Trip Advisor, along with many of the other online review platforms were here to stay, and any would-be guest house proprietor just had to accept it.

Our reviews were reasonable – but nothing to write home about. After nearly ten years, we had 4 out of 5 stars, but were no competition for the 5-star establishments who prided themselves on both the quantity and quality of their reviews, and made a point of announcing this at every given opportunity:

'Please spend a few moments reading the wonderful reviews we have on Trip Advisor' was one of our favourites. One place had a huge canvas banner with "No.1 on Trip Advisor" printed in block capitals. They must have really been pissed off several months later when they were overtaken by another place. Perhaps they sold the banner to them at half price?

At the last count we had 4 "terrible" reviews which, after 10 years of trading, to only have 4 people who thought you were terrible, is quite an achievement, I personally think!

Establishments in the No.1 spot usually milk it for what it's worth – and quite rightly so. Several owners work very hard to maintain their high ranking, and that usually involves handing out trip advisor cards to every departing customer asking them to post a (hopefully) glowing review.

To my mind this must be incredibly difficult. Of the dozens and dozens of guests checking in and out each week, to see every one as a "potential reviewer" and therefore, de facto, a possible negative reviewer as well must be emotionally as well as physically draining. Nothing should be out of place and lord help them if there was a small curly hair in the shower. The only way I can think of describing what it must be like, is to live in a house with white carpets and not dare to have a glass of red wine! I can't begin to imagine the fawning and gushing necessary in order to achieve such arbitrary recognition or, worse still, comprehend the childhood trauma suffered to necessitate such self-esteem boosting!

It was something we didn't need to worry about.

Invariably, a negative review reflects the mood and emotional state of the reviewer: a mirror reflecting their own psychological state of mind if you like. Some people are just negative and appear to walk around with a dark cloud above them, influencing the way they see everything, and in turn, how people react to them, whereas others are the exact opposite: full of positivity.

Some run up to the front door full of enthusiasm and positivity, and you know that they will enjoy their stay in Harrogate. On the other hand, others will arrive surrounded by the large, dark grey cloud. They bring negativity with them and from the moment they set foot in the hall, you know there will be problems.

Now I can stand back, be a little more detached and realise that these people are negative for a reason, and that chances are that it's got absolutely nothing to do with you.

As an interesting experiment of sorts, for a period of a few weeks (couldn't keep it up that long!), I did my utmost to be as kind and helpful to these sorts of people, and the transformation this brings is quite remarkable. Whereas a few years ago I'd be spitting venom at them aka Basil Fawlty style, I tried to show a little more empathy.

Some of the kindest comments in our guest book were made by such people and I suppose the one thing that binds us together as humans, regardless of the job we do to make our living, is that we all interact with each other and we all play a minor role in other people's life stories as well as playing the leading role in our own.

Alternatively, a bad review could simply be that the customer was told to 'Fuck off and not stay here again!' by the owner.

Well, to be accurate, I did not actually tell him to 'Fuck off'.

Our first "Terrible" review was courtesy of a regular guest staying with us for the eighth or ninth time. It was during a very busy trade show where demand for rooms was extremely high and many establishments were charging up to double the normal room rate – and then some more.

This chap had enjoyed a good deal with us, and as we began to realise just how little he was actually paying, we decided it was time to do something about it. It would be unfair to submit an invoice without prior warning, so I simply handed him an invoice with what we thought the going room rate should have been – minus what he was actually paying (to enable him to see the hefty discount he was receiving).

Unfortunately, the gentleman was in a tired an irritable mood when he checked out; he hadn't had a particularly good show and his gout had been troubling him throughout the week (eggs for breakfast, lots of standing and drinking red wine in the evenings). Instead of smiling and patting me on the back, grateful for the several hundred pounds discount he'd been receiving, he started shouting and calling me unprofessional!

I thought I had gone about it in a professional way, but obviously there was a lot about corporate etiquette I had yet to learn.

Before long, a very lively discussion was taking place and eight years of hosting this irritable, volatile blowhard was bubbling up to the surface, and the conversation ended with me asking him to find alternative accommodation elsewhere the following year. Technically, therefore, I did not tell him to "Fuck off" (but it was certainly never far from my mind!).

Another "Terrible" review was from a customer who I just managed to refrain from telling him to "Fuck off". Not because I abhor bad language, but because I had only just told him we would not tolerate bad language ourselves in our own guest house!

This chap made an incredible scene on departure, threatening to leave a stinking review informing the world and his brother about the appalling way we treated him, but of course when the eventual review appeared, he hadn't quite fully explained what had happened: selective memory of sorts, perhaps?

Over an hour after check-out time, he was still fast asleep, and despite several polite attempts to wake him, we were just met by grunts and teenage like retorts of, 'Whatever! Whatever! Stop hassling me. I'll be out when I'm ready.'

This went on for an hour and a half after check-out time, and we were due to be somewhere thirty minutes before the chap had even made an appearance; we eventually had to cancel our event.

Out of desperation, I unlocked his single room with the master key, saw a woman in his bed and was greeted by shouts of, 'What the fuck are you doing in my room? Get the fuck out! Is this how you fucking treat your guests?'

I made one big mistake at this point. I pointed out that such bad language was unacceptable in our establishment (more or less true), but I also said that I didn't want his type staying here again.

Only when I said this did I realise I'd inadvertently created a bit of a problem for myself: the guy was black.

That's when he launched into a tirade of just wait until Trip Advisor hears of this!

Fortunately, I was able to explain my side of the story to "Trip Advisor" and the review about the bigoted, perverted racist was removed.

How am I doing? Have I told enough horror stories to persuade any would be guest house proprietor to stick to their 9-to-5 job? Is the dream already a faded post-it not even sticking on the wall properly?

Well, seeing that you have stuck with me thus far, I do have a slight confession to make. I need to make all readers aware of the 99% rule.

Anyone working with general public, in whatever capacity, will understand this "unofficial" rule. Basically, it states that 99% of the people you deal with will be lovely, warm, friendly, normal people who are a pleasure to meet. In short, they are not problem people! This obviously means that if the majority of guests fall into this category, then only 1% of guests are a problem! Dr Johns (Chapter 1), the wine drinking, gout suffering corporate blowhard and the black good-time guy were therefore in this very small minority!

When I sat down to write this chapter, I thought it would be the easiest one to write; certainly the one with the most material – but ironically, it has turned out to be quite the opposite. When I think long and hard about the "problem" guests we'd had, then you realise that even these characters are not really "bad" in the literal definition of the word. On another day, I'd perhaps even enjoy having a pint with any of them in a pub somewhere (OK, perhaps a G&T with the doctor), but it puts everything in perspective and is a timely reminder just how privileged we are to be able to meet so many different, interesting people in our daily lives.

Admittedly, not all of the 99% will walk out and write glowing, excellent reviews. Some may be just too polite to tell you what they are actually thinking, though the majority will be simply just thinking "that was all right" and leave it at that. Perhaps we should start to hand our guests Trip Advisor cards! We could even tell them all "Excellent" reviews received will be put in a prize draw and the winner will receive a free one-night stay.

(And please no one email me to suggest the runner up wins a two night stay!).

Even problems can be re-categorised at a later date. While some are really big problems, many turn out to be just minor hiccups – and often amusing ones at that. This was certainly the case when Trudy and Nelson "checked" in.

We had been expecting an American couple who were due to land at Leeds Bradford Airport at around seven o'clock one evening. We knew the flight had been delayed, so took a gamble and went out to meet some friends for a couple of hours.

We left a note for the guests together with the key to the front door hanging in our porch. It was not an ideal way of greeting guests, especially ones from across the Atlantic, but decided we would not be prisoners to the business.

When we returned, however, we got far more than even we bargained for! We saw the lights were on in our private living area and the TV was going full blast.

I opened to door to find two elderly people sitting there, drinking wine and nibbling nuts and crisps.

'Oh hi there!' said a large American lady, 'We got your note, thanks! We just helped ourselves to wine and found these nibbles in the cupboard! We guessed that's the way you guys operate here! Oh so cute!'

We realised that the door to our private area had not been locked, and so we could hardly blame the Americans, though how we were going to explain to them politely that they were trespassing on private property after an eight hour trans-Atlantic flight was a difficult one.

'Fuck off! You're in our living room?' – No. There had to be a more subtle approach.

We sat down with the guests and introduced ourselves. We even got two more wine glasses and joined them for a drink – it was our wine after all!

We chatted for a while, and when the Americans asked where we lived we got the chance to put them straight.

They were really mortified when they found out what they had done, and then it was our turn to feel guilty!

Luckily we all saw the funny side, and in a way, it got their visit off to a great start, and when they returned to state side, they left a lovely review:

Jo and Mike

Thank you for your delightful hospitality and kindness. We've both very much appreciated all you've done. Best of luck, Trudy and Nelson.

PS Thank you for the wine and the nuts!

Unfortunately, not all our American guests were as "easy" as Trudy and Nelson were.

A large American gentleman walked in, and after shaking my hand in an energetic way, took his coat off and handed it to me before looking incredulously up and down at the paintings and furniture in the reception hall.

'This is a…er…quaint little place you have here.'

'Thanks,' I replied, trying to be as professional as possible, though sometimes Jo did wonder how wearing ripped jeans and a rugby shirt with dried paint on the back counted as professional.

I was unsure as to whether or not the guy was being complimentary or sarcastic; I obviously had not grasped the essentials of American humour and wondered if I ever would.

'Breakfast is served in this room from seven thirty onwards and we stop around nine.'

'I was hoping to have breakfast at 9:30!'

'Well, that's perhaps a little bit late, but if you like we could compromise and go for nine fifteen?'

'That will have to do then.'

'Let me show you to your room. Is this the only suitcase you have?'

'Lord no. I have another two in the car; maybe you can arrange to have them brought up to my room?'

'We'll sort that out soon,' I said, wondering what the logical end to this conversation will be, though somehow guessed that it would involve me dragging two heavy suitcases up two flights of stairs. We did not have to wait long to speak to our new American guest as the door to his room slammed shut and we heard him march downstairs and towards the reception area.

'I can't seem to find the phone in my room.'

'That's because there isn't a phone in the room,' replied Jo, making every effort to remain cool and professional in front or a very objectionable guest, even though he had just arrived.

'What, no phone! What kind of a hotel is this, god dammit?'

'This is not a hotel; it is in fact a guest house. It is our house! You are a guest in our house! Had you paid to stay in a hotel you would have more facilities, including a phone in the room, but you would be paying significantly more than you are paying during your stay here!'

The American guest mumbled something and stormed back to his room.

'What shall we do about his suitcases?'

'Let the bastard get them himself!'

Just as we had sat down to watch the evening news, the telephone rang. It was the wife of the American guest.

'May I speak to Ray?' she enquired.

I thought about lecturing her on the importance of not hogging our one business line, but decided that it would be far simpler just to take the phone up to his room.

I knocked very tentatively on his door.

'Yes?'

'Ray, sorry to bother you, but your wife is on the hotel phone.'

The door opened and an arm poked out to grab the receiver. I handed it over and watched the door slam shut in my face. Should I stay here and wait for the call to finish or go back downstairs in the hope that "Ray" would bring it back down when he had finished talking to his wife.

****

'Fancy a cuppa?'

'What time are we supposed to be going out?'

'Another hour or so; I'm having a warm drink anyway!'

'Please, then.'

Jo went to the kitchen and I looked at my watch. The American guest had been talking for over half an hour, this was not on! What if someone were trying to ring through and make a reservation?

I ran upstairs and put my ear to the door. All quiet! I knocked.

'Hello! Hello!'

Once again the door opened slightly and a face peered at me.

'I was wondering if you'd finished talking to your wife.'

The American mumbled something and passed the phone to me; he made no further comment.

We went out to the pub that evening, and no doubt much of the conversation revolved around the fact that some guests, for whatever reason, are not that friendly and we just had to accept it when, suddenly, my mobile rang. Whenever we go out, we switch to call divert so we can receive calls and not miss out on any potential bookings – or at least that's the theory.

I remember one afternoon on a short break to Cornwall, we were at the Eden Project and yes, the mobile was on call divert.

I had to deal with a cacophony of sales calls from electrical suppliers to web site developers in the Rainforest Biome, with the telephone constantly slipping down my sweat laded face as I struggled to open the reservations book in the hope that one of the calls might be an actual booking!

Luckily, the pub wasn't as warm as the Rainforest Biome.

'Oh hi,' went the voice, and I knew instantly who it was. 'May I speak to Ray?'

When I pointed out that we were not at the guest house I received another verbal assault from his wife this time on how inconvenient it was for her to communicate with her husband via an establishment that was so utterly incompetent and behind the times. Needless to say, I managed to "hold it" together – despite already having drunk two and a half pints of Timothy Taylor's Landlord and further aggravated by half a dozen friends all enjoying this unexpected side show!

Like anything in life, running a guest house has its ups and downs. The fantastic people we met outnumbered the difficult or challenging ones, and we really didn't have much to complain about – though Jo did remind me about being woken up in the middle of the night once.

In fact, one night the telephone went twice: a drunken man rang at 2:30 in the morning to ask if we had a spare room, and Booking.com rang from America at 3:30 a.m. to advise us that a reservation over two months away had been altered; the guest wanted to let us know that he required a vegetarian breakfast.

I think I had a bit of a rant to the American girl on the other end of the line, but apologised to the drunken guy which irritated Jo.

'You don't seem at all upset that they woke you up in the middle of the night; you even said sorry to him! He should have said sorry to you for waking us both up!'

'I know. Come on, try to get some sleep.'

'I can't sleep now; I'm wide awake. Shall I make a cup of tea?'

With that, Jo got out of bed and made her way up to the kitchen to make us both a cup of tea. I was wide awake now as well. There was no getting away from the fact that this was one of the downsides to running a Guest House. Everyone thought we were a hotel and employed someone to sit at a desk throughout the night just in case people like that phoned at half past two in the morning on the off chance that we had a spare room.

This certainly had annoyed Jo. Yes, we've been woken up several times during the night since we had taken over at Holland House, but it was not a frequent occurrence and it would only happen on a Saturday night during very busy periods.

I heard Jo coming down the stairs with the tea, knew she was not happy and I knew what was coming next

'We can't even have a good night's sleep without being disturbed by some drunken idiot. Whose bloody idea was it to run a Guest House in the first place?'

Chapter 12
Japanese Guests

Our friendship groups extended across the North Sea to Germany and Holland, where we had both lived and worked before returning to the UK. We both agreed that we would like to create a guest house welcoming to overseas visitors. One of the first things we did was to have our web site translated into several different European languages, and even considered offering continental breakfasts instead of the traditional full English option. However, after a few years, we came to realise that the majority of our visitors came from the North East and that the most of them wanted a good old fashioned fry up first thing in the morning.

We both spoke the languages of the countries we had lived in, though Jo was much more of a classical linguist than me. For me, it was all about communication and people – getting your point across in whatever way possible. Whilst I was able to communicate reasonably well (especially after a few pints of beer), my grammar was atrocious. I had never bothered to learn the articles and don't know or couldn't have cared less what an interrogative or relative pronoun was in English – let alone Dutch or German.

Jo, on the other hand, preferred to master the grammar of any language she learnt before she dared to express any feelings or views.

I often brought this difference up in discussion and had a theory that women were predominantly programmed to master the small minutiae and evolution had provided them with a keen eye for detail. Maybe this was natural selection at work; ensuring the suitability of the meat brought in from the hunt? I found it difficult applying social Darwinism on a day to day basis, though when Jo shouted down at me telling me that I'd missed something in one of the rooms, I sometimes wished I was out with some of my mates enjoying the camaraderie of a "virtual" hunt of some description.

'It's all about detail,' she'd say to me. 'That's what people look at when they walk into a room – the small little touches that make all the difference.'

Detail confused and bewildered me. I spent half a day trying to master how to fold a toilet roll to make it more presentable for our guests. I ended up reducing a decent sized roll to half its size before my supervisor passed it!

And as for playing the supervisor role, she only had to run her fingers under taps to see that I hadn't cleaned the sink thoroughly and that the mirrors were never streak free when I had been in an en-suite.

'But how do you get them so clean?' I'd plead.

'It might help using a clean cloth!' she'd often say, holding up a filthy sopping wet rag that was only fit for cleaning the end of a rod after it had unblocked the drains.

Let's tear ourselves away from the minutiae of cleaning and focus on the more positive side of running a guest house, and undoubtedly, one of the biggest advantages is the opportunity to meet many delightful people from all over – both this country and further afield. We have hosted guests from neighbouring France, Holland and Germany, and of course from down under, Kiwis and Ozzies.

One of the most amusing, though at the time quite worrying tales came from a lovely girl from Japan and an amorous Libyan, drunk (often quite literally) on the freedom the West had to offer.

The Japanese girl was a long term guest. She was over to improve her English and attended a language school during the day. Her parents had insisted she stay in a small hotel; they did not want her to be alone with a strange family. We saw very little of her as her work ethic was incredibly strong, though of course whenever we bumped into her along the corridor she would take the opportunity to practice her English. The Libyan man was over for exactly the same reason, though he made sure he engaged in conversations every evening with English people (or to be more accurate, English girls) in pubs and nightclubs. There was little contact between the two, and for several weeks things went along quite nicely.

The problem came to a head one evening when my wife happened to be away for a few days visiting her sister in The Netherlands. I was sitting alone when the Japanese girl came down, knocked politely on the door and asked if she could speak to me about a delicate matter. I just assumed it was her ultra-polite way of initiating a discussion on the split infinitive, but soon realised that it was more serious than that.

'I have big problem, with Sami', she said. 'He sent me text message'.

She passed her mobile to me and showed me the message he had sent her.

The message went: 'Come to my room. Wear something sexy'.

The poor girl was beside herself. This was a massive shock to her and she clearly didn't know what to do next. I reassured her as best as I could and said that I would have a word with the guy and try to sort things out. Even this however, was not going to be enough and already she was talking about going to find somewhere else to stay.

The next day, I phoned the language school and played at being Henry Kissinger. The administrators agreed with me that this could all be smoothed over and that it was more than likely a big misunderstanding.

Misunderstanding or not, it was clearly going to be a case of either Sami goes or I go for the Japanese girl!

Eventually, I caught up with Sami and we sat down and had a man to man sort of chat. I managed to convince him that he had not only really upset the girl, but that she was now so frightened about staying in the same guest house as him that one of them would have to go! I then hinted that perhaps it would be best if he did the right thing by writing a letter of apology and finding an alternative hotel or guest house. I even offered to help him find suitable accommodation elsewhere.

The letter and the news of Sami's impending move helped calm things down, and until the day of his moving out, things almost returned to normal.

When I went up to Sami's room on the day he was due to leave, he had packed all his bags and was in the process of writing a letter of apology to me as well.

The English wasn't that good but the gist of the text was that he was sorry for what he had done and he wanted to tell me that he was a good boy. When he looked up at me, I could tell he had been crying, so I put my arm around his shoulders, patted him and told him that we are learning all the time!

He soon cheered up and I dropped him off at a friend's hotel a couple of miles away. As Sami got out of the car, I winked at him and said 'Sami, you are a good boy but you wanted to be a naughty boy, didn't you?'

He laughed and hurried up to his room. He evidently had to hurry as he'd arranged to meet a couple of other fellow Libyan students at the pub that evening.

However, perhaps our most colourful Japanese guest was Taro, a young and ambitious business student who was eager to carve a future for himself in politics. To help facilitate this, Taro enrolled in a 6 month intensive English course, and booked into our guest house for the duration of his studies. He was the ideal guest: hardworking, extremely polite and courteous as well as very, very, amusing.

However, not all the other guests found Taro as amusing as we did.

Early on in Taro's stay with us, one customer complained about the strange sound throughout the night. We had no idea what the sound could be and thoroughly investigated the room during the day, but found nothing which could have explained any strange noise. We explained our findings to our guest and hoped that whatever the noise had been was a one off and that he would have an undisturbed night's sleep.

Unfortunately for the poor man, the next night was if anything more disturbed than the previous night, though being forewarned, our guest was able to pin point the source of the noise a little more accurately.

'It's definitely coming from the room below me,' explained our guest.

'Mmmm, that's Taro's room,' we explained. 'Our Japanese guest.'

We said that we would have a word with him and kindly ask him to be a little more considerate to other customers – especially during the early hours of the morning.

We had a chat with Taro and what we found out was quite incredulous! As well as studying English full time, Taro had his own web based company in Japan, and because of the time difference, conducted most of his business in the early hours of the morning. Sometimes, he explained to us. He wouldn't finish until 4 or 5 o'clock in the morning, and would have just an hour or so sleep before showering and changing the business hat for the student hat!

The noise had been the low drone of Taro's Japanese over the computer, and obviously the muffled sounds of the Japanese language came over as something very strange to our other guest. We suggested that if Taro were to continue business conversations well into the early hours he should perhaps come downstairs and use the guest room rather than disturbing other guests.

Taro was extremely hard-working, and the nightly business dealings didn't seem to affect his thirst for the English language: whenever we'd bump into him, he would always have a question about some aspect of grammar which invariably, we weren't able to answer (or at least I wasn't!).

One thing did puzzle us though.

Despite the very hard-working and serious nature of our guest, his room contained a wide and varied collection of spirits which he had lined up in almost military precision along the end wall, starting with the largest bottle – a bottle of a peaty malt whisky, and ending up with a small, squat and chunky bottle of dark tequila. There were six or seven bottles in total and nothing appeared to have been drunk from any of the bottles.

Perhaps he had had put them there for decoration? A subtle reminder of what could become of him if he were to jettison his Pacific Rim work ethic in favour of more hedonistic European attitudes?

The question of the bottles was shortly answered one Friday evening.

Taro had returned from college after a particularly hard week of tests in preparation for his IELTS English examination. I asked him what he had planned for that evening.

Taro's reply was, 'tonight I will get into alcoholic stupor!'

This rather surprising answer intrigued me and I was determined to find out just what exactly the "stupor" entailed. He

122

informed me that he would systematically sample all the drinks in his room, going from bottle to bottle until he was unable to drink any more.

I wished him a "pleasant" evening and didn't see Taro until the next day when he appeared for breakfast looking rather bleary eyed and the worse for wear. He said very little and ate even less. He returned to his room only to appear an hour or so later looking a little more refreshed and smiled at me as he went out into the cold November air and, rubbing his hands said, 'Now, stupor over!'

Business as usual for our Japanese guest I suspected.

Of course, apart from the array of alcoholic drinks (which were decreasing in volume on a weekly basis) the main space in his room was his laptop and his camera. In fact, Taro rarely ventured anywhere without his precious camera and would stop and take photographs of the most unlikely of objects.

He asked if he could watch me cooking breakfast one morning – something which broke all the health, safety and hygiene rules, but in a defiant attack against the country's obsession with health and safety regulations, I agreed to his request. He took photographs of the bacon under the grill, the tomatoes on the griddle and the sausages in the frying pan.

He did insist on setting his camera up on a tripod next to eggs being fried. I suggested he not get the camera too close in case the fat from the eggs splashed it. He consulted the manual and set it on lapse mode whereby the camera took a photograph every few seconds or so to enable him to show his friends back in Japan the varying stages of an egg being fried.

Mmmm. Perhaps this is what they would look at when getting into a "stupor" on Friday nights!

Taro stayed with us over the Christmas period.

In fact, he was our only guest.

We had contemplated going away, but thought we would discuss the situation with him. We explained that, whilst he would be very welcome to spend Christmas with us, the typical Christmas day was really a big anti-climax after all the media hype that spews out of our TV sets in the six or seven weeks in the run up to the festive season.

'We just really eat, and watch TV all day,' we explained to him. 'In fact,' I added, 'it's quite a boring event.'

Taro's typically unsurprising reply was, 'I wish to experience typical boring Christmas day!'

So that was that. Taro would be staying with us over Christmas.

We thought we had better do something special to help make this not quite the typical boring Christmas so many of us have grown to love (or hate!), so one thing we decided on was to take him to the carol service on Christmas eve at Ripon Cathedral.

He was very excited about this and of course made sure he had a few extra memory cards with him for the event.

We arrived at the cathedral to find just about the last few seats in an otherwise very large congregation. The seats had somewhat restricted access behind one of the large gothic columns, but I guessed if it were a toss-up between having a better view or the roof caving in on us, there was only one real choice.

For Taro however, the restricted view was a major hindrance in his quest for yet another catalogue of photographs, and half way during the service he got up and went for a "walk about" in the cathedral – much to my discomfort. My wife whispered something about leaving him and that he would be alright, but I sang the next few carols in a slightly agitated, discorded and off-key sort of way.

During the key sermon given by the bishop, I was aware of "flashes of light" going off in the church and the turning of heads among the people surrounding us.

Of course, this was not any form of divine intervention, but a mystical light from the orient in the form of Taro's camera.

He had now worked his way round the church and was back near us when he spotted the crib with the life size models of Mary, Joseph, the baby Jesus and the shepherds. This intrigued him enormously and he at once darted up to the crib, and in a rather loud and incredulous voice let out a high pitched and very discernible 'Whooooooooo!'

He then started to take what seemed like hundreds of photographs of the crib, by which time there were sniggers and giggles coming from everyone around us.

We managed to get through the service singing the last hymn *Once in Royal David's City* without too many flashes of Eastern technological mysticism disrupting the service. And as the

Bishop, followed by the rest of the cassocks and surplices, made their way down the main aisle to the exit, we assumed Taro was lost in the crowd and that we would only find him after everyone had left the building.

What I saw next made me want to curl up in a ball and hide away next to baby Jesus himself in the life sized crib.

The bishop, complete with mitre and crozier, had been made to stand still in the middle of the aisle by Taro, doing a very creditable impersonation of a traffic policeman in a heavily congested Tokyo high street – holding his right hand up to signal stop whilst flashing away with the camera in the other hand. He then waved on the procession, taking more photographs of the altar servers as they passed by.

We made our way out of the cathedral and waited until virtually everyone had gone before re-joining a very excited Taro jabbering away in Japanese on his mobile to his parents. We guessed he was speaking of his experience because in between the indecipherable words we heard "Christmas" mentioned more than a few times.

This obviously had been a great experience for him and one he would not forget in a hurry.

Nor would I.

Christmas day was the usual giving and receiving of presents, preparing, cooking and eating the meal and falling asleep in front of the TV after the Queen's speech.

Taro joined in enthusiastically and quite liked the crackers; he put the paper hat on his head but didn't quite get the joke!

Before he retired to his room, he stood up to make a formal announcement. He said he wished to thank us for allowing him to partake in our "typical boring Christmas tradition" and made his way back to his room either to watch Eastenders' Christmas special, phone a business contact in Tokyo or simply get into "stupor"!

Taro decided to do some travelling for the rest of the Christmas holidays, and the day after Boxing Day he headed off to Germany for a few days, also giving us a few days of well-earned rest and time to spend with a few friends. Whenever we met in the pub, one of the inevitable conversations was what our recent experiences had been, so much time was spent recalling the exploits of Taro in Ripon Cathedral. Little did we know that in our absence, he was still going to provide us with more entertaining tales to amuse friends in the weeks and months that lay ahead.

When he returned, he was keen to show us some of the photographs he had taken on his whistle stop tour of Germany a la Japanese style. This involved jumping off a train, taking a photograph and jumping back on again in preparation for the next destination. We saw a photograph of him eating a hamburger in Hamburg, a frankfurter in Frankfurt and holding a bottle of Heinz tomato ketchup outside Mainz central station; whilst I got the significance of the hamburger and frankfurter, the Heinz connection left me a little puzzled. He did, however, recall his most amusing story in Berlin (where there was, incidentally, no photo of him eating a Berliner).

He had been in a Christmas market and he was excited to recall the wonderful fairy tale atmosphere including the snow, the lights, organ music and the smells of mulled wine and bratwurst. He told me he looked up to the starry sky and there, in front of him was a girl from his English class. He said it could have been a scene from a love story film. The snow, the music, the lights and of course, the girl.

I winked at Taro and asked him if he liked the girl.

'No, of course not!' he replied. 'I hate girl!'

Chapter 13
Some Interesting Paying (and Non-Paying!) Guests

I was busy looking through the reservations diary for the last few weeks of the year. Apart from one last conference, all our guests were over for a variety of reasons: work, shopping, the annual pantomime as well as the usual festive round of Christmas parties and celebrations.

We had only one guest in the previous night, and Jo thought that booking would turn out to be a hoax one.

A gentleman had made a booking by telephone and said that his name was "Mycock".

Now, had I taken the phone call, I would have thought nothing of it, but Jo, being Dutch and never having heard such a name before was convinced it was a hoax call.

'Surely no one could be called that!'

She nearly rang my mate to tell him to stop taking the "you know what", but for some strange reason didn't. He was notorious for his irreverence and high antics; just the sort of thing he would do.

'Do you reckon it's Beany?'

Before we could argue any further, the confusion abated as a gentleman walked into the reception area and introduced himself as Mr Mycock.

He was a very pleasant and perfectly normal guy. He and his girlfriend just fancied a bit of luxury after walking in the Dales for a couple of days. She was a history teacher and had been over in York doing some reconnaissance for a GCSE field trip later on in the year

Our guests had a pleasant evening in Harrogate and after a good nights' sleep. came down for breakfast.

'Good morning!'

Mr Mycock and his girlfriend looked up and smiled at us.

'Good morning.'

'Been doing some walking in The Dales, I hear?'

He explained how he'd been walking up in Swaledale, which was one of my favourite parts of the Dales.

'Did you stay there?'

'Yes,' replied Mr Mycock, 'in a small village called Muker.'

'Have a drink in The Farmer's Arms by any chance?'

'Why, yes!' replied their shocked guest.

'We always visit there whenever we get the chance! Small world, isn't it?'

Jo brought a coffee and a tea in for the guests and indicated to me to get back in the kitchen and prepare to do an order.

Jo slapped a post-it on the work surface in front of me.

'One Full English and a scrambled egg on toast.'

I sprang into action and before long, a Holland House Full English and a scrambled egg, made according to Margaret's secret recipe, was ready for service.

Jo took their meals to the dining room. I cleared the kitchen, and as soon as I was done, wandered through to the dining room, keen to continue the discussion about this and that. I enjoyed this part of the day, and hand on heart, would say it was the main reason why I wanted to run a Guest House in the first place.

'Any more toast?'

'No thanks that was great!' replied our guest.

'What are your plans for today?'

'Well, we were thinking of visiting the Black Sheep Brewery Centre. Have you been there?'

'Masham! Great place! Must admit, I prefer Theakston's to Black Sheep, but the centre is worth a visit! Great meals as well!'

'Right, sounds like that's the place to head to.'

I suggested that it be might be worth contacting the centre just to make sure they were open. I brought the telephone out to the hall and dialled the number I had found on the internet.

'Yes, good morning, it's Mike from Holland House in Harrogate. I'm ringing on behalf of some guests; are you open today?'

I nodded to them, suggesting that it was open.

'Do they want to have a guided tour of the brewery?'

Mr Mycock nodded.

'Yes please; two tickets please. Err, yes, their surname…'

Oh my god, I froze. I knew the name, but I also knew that if I said it I'd burst into uncontrollable laughter. This was stupid. I'm a mature fifty-something year old and not a giggling schoolboy who sniggers at every smutty word he hears. I looked up at Mr Mycock, and hoped the pregnant pause might reboot the charged atmosphere.

I was biting my lip.

'Sorry your surname is?'

'Mycock.'

'Mycock,' I spluttered – now quite red in the face.

'I BEG YOUR PADON!' shrieked the lady at the other end of the telephone.

That was it. I just let out an uncontrollable howl.

Mr Mycock turned round and gave a knowing sigh. He looked at his girlfriend and said, 'I knew we should have used your name.'

No one knew where to look or what to do, and after a few polite exchanges and good wishes, the couple went up to their room to collect their luggage and check out for the first, and probably the last time, from Holland House.

'Got to tell that one to Beany!' laughed Jo.

'Even he will not believe that one!'

Just as poor Mr Mycock departed, another milestone guest was about to arrive.

Jo asked me to see what was going on in the car park; she could hear a lot of noise and commotion.

'You've still got another two yards!' exclaimed a frustrated lady as her husband tried to park an old Austin Westminster into one of the remaining spaces.

The driver inched back at a tediously slow pace and the poor lady looked up at me pleadingly.

'Can I help at all?'

'I think we're nearly there.' She replied, 'just another half a yard and that should do it.'

'The car's fine as it is,' I informed the guest. 'No one will be moving them until after the weekend, so you don't need to worry too much.'

An elderly gentleman climbed out of the car and introduced himself.

'Good morning young man!'

I went round to the other side and offered my hand to the gentleman.

'Mike. Welcome to Holland House. Can I give you a hand with your luggage?'

'Oh, that would be very kind of you,' answered his wife, who was already busy sorting out what to take and what to leave behind in the vehicle.

'It's a good job I've got her to sort me out, isn't it?' said the driver.

I saw that there were two largish leather suitcases, and so grabbed hold of the both of them.

'Here, let me take these for you.'

With that, the party made their way to the house.

'I'll bring you in through the tradesman entrance,' I said, 'won't need to contend with the steep steps at the front!'

The couple thanked me for my help and said they wanted breakfast at about 8:30.

'My wife will be attending the Christmas Fair, but I'll be spending most of my time here – apart from when I'm in the pub of course!'

I laughed. 'We've got some great pubs here. The Old Bell Tavern has some great beers and was Bill Clinton's favourite pub when he visited Harrogate. Hales bar is a very atmospheric place too, with a lot of character. They filmed the trailer for the film Chariots of Fire there.'

'Sounds very promising! I shall look forward to the imbibing this evening. My wife is essentially here to purchase Christmas presents; something I find tremendously tedious. However, I write, so my days will be spent profitably – at least I hope to have something to show for my time spent in Harrogate. After breakfast, I shall return to my room.'

I was very impressed. We'd only had one writer staying with us. He'd written a true crime novel. He had mentioned this to the group staying at Holland House for the annual Harrogate Crime Writers Festival, but was disappointed to hear that no one had ever heard of him!

We had a regular guest who stayed with us for this Festival: He was a book dealer, and our nearest claim to fame. He came down for breakfast one morning looking rather the worse for wear. He informed me that he and Ian Rankin had finished off a bottle of scotch between them and had not gone to bed until four in the morning!

After the writer and his wife had finished breakfast the next day, I offered him the choice of returning to his room or staying in the dining room.

'You're quite welcome to stay down here. I can leave a table clear for you so you can set your stall out so to speak and, it's much warmer here than in the bedroom – the heating goes off at about 10:30.'

'That's most kind of you,' the writer informed me, 'but I think I'd prefer to stay in my room; it's much quieter there and I find that I do need to concentrate much more than I used to.'

'Absolutely,' I agreed.

'Yes, everything's up there and I'd rather not disturb my pile as it tends to disturb my thought processes – if you see what I mean?'

'Yes of course. How long have you been writing?'

'Oh, most of my life really.'

I was impressed and wondered what he was writing. Was it Fiction or non-fiction? Crime or Romance? Maybe he was even a well-known author staying incognito – searching for material, characters and ideas for his next bestseller?

On the final morning, before he checked out, my curiosity got the better of me and I was itching to find out what he was actually writing.

The couple came down for breakfast and I waited for a lull in the service to pop into the dining room to chat with guests. I made my way over to the couple and first chatted to his wife asking her about her shopping and where they both ate the previous evening.

I then turned to her husband as he was eating his breakfast.

'I really must ask what you are actually writing.'

He put his knife and fork down on the table, looked up to me, and said, 'My Christmas cards!'

Jo rolled around in complete hysterics when she heard that! 'He was writing Christmas cards!!! I thought he was a writer and he was only writing Christmas cards! Oh so priceless!'

The reader will by now be aware that the majority of encounters with guests are positive and often very funny. In fact, it was probably meeting the Christmas card "writer" that convinced me that some of these tales should be recorded somehow, and from that day I kept a diary – just recalling events, people and situations as they developed. I remember thinking that although I have a very good imagination, there is no way I could have made up this particular story and I never tire of sharing it with friends.

Another tale refers to a non-paying guest we have – or at least we think we have.

This story developed over several years and started one weekend after talking to some delightful people over for a reunion. They had thoroughly enjoyed their stay and we were chatting about this and that when the lady said something that brought silence to the few of us left in the dining room.

She told us that during the night she had felt a distinct chill in the room and looking up had seen a young girl standing at the foot of the bed. She said she didn't feel at all frightened or threatened in any way. She must have been there for only a few seconds, but it was very real.

We were naturally shocked at hearing this. We had lived in the house for several years, but to be fair, had only slept in that particular bedroom a couple of times.

I must admit I felt a bit spooked when I went into the room to change the bedding, but everything seemed normal to me. I put the TV on (turned up the volume quite high as well!), and then thought nothing more about the event for several months.

The next time the young girl was mentioned was after a couple of ladies had been staying. They had been to see a Pink Floyd tribute band playing at the International Conference Theatre and, being a Pink Floyd fan, enjoyed chatting to them about the show.

I remember laughing after they told me how many audience members were on crutches, in a wheelchair or had a Zimmer frame. One of the ladies also, suddenly and without warning, told us that both her and her friend thought the house was haunted.

They were quick to add that they thought the house had a lovely warm mellow feel to it, but they had definitely experienced something in their room the previous night. What they had experienced was unclear except to say one of the ladies thought she saw a young girl walking across the room and then this girl suddenly vanished.

We were intrigued, and obviously did not doubt the integrity of the guests who claimed to have seen this young girl.

A good friend and fellow guest house owner, Derek, also recalled the time when he had walked into one of the bedrooms only to have seen a lady sitting at the end of the bed. He told me she was real – but didn't look real, and he told me how he stared at her for quite a few seconds until she slowly started to fade away.

I was reassured to have heard Derek's story. It convinced me that there might be something here after all. Whatever it was, it was not in any way threatening or sinister, and after a while, we were beginning to grow quite intrigued about our "non-paying" guest.

During a conversation we had with friends, someone suggested we should get in touch with a gentleman called Gordon, who lived in York. He was supposed to be an expert in sorting problems like this out – although at the time we did not think it was a problem as such.

We eventually met up with Gordon, and his delightful wife, Gaynor and arranged for them to come and spend a night at the guest house – as our guests obviously! They were both mediums and Gordon specialised in clearing out unwanted 'entities' as he called them.

I expected to meet a gentleman dressed in a black cloak and top hat, but was surprised when he eventually arrived wearing a pair of jeans and a Wakefield Trinity rugby league sweatshirt.

We hit it off immediately with this delightful couple and before long were chatting about all sorts of things when Gordon announced he would like to go to their room to freshen up and change his shirt.

We gave him the key to the room and didn't see him for another twenty minutes or so.

When he came down, he was smiling and said that our customers had been correct. There was a young girl here who spent a great deal of time in that room. He also explained that she had not lived in the house before, but that she was in some way attached to you two – looking directly at Jo and myself!

We were completely shocked at this and it took us a while to gain our composure and even then, neither of us was able to say anything.

Gaynor asked an interesting question.

She wanted to know if Jo had had a miscarriage at any point,

We thought about this long and hard. Jo remembered a time when she thought she might have had a miscarriage, but it was only after a month or so, so even she wasn't really that sure.

Gordon went on to tell us that the girl's name was Kay. He described her in great detail to us. Interestingly, he could have been describing our other daughter who lived in Spain – who, of course, they had never met.

We got on really well together and they suggested they return at some point in the future and they would bring a friend with them, Christine, who was a psychic artist who would try to get us a portrait of "Kay".

The next mention of Kay was by far the most intriguing.

A young couple from Wales together with their daughter came to stay with us. She was a very pretty dark girl with masses of jet black curly hair. She had a most unusual Celtic name which unfortunately I failed to take a note of.

When they came down for breakfast, we were chatting about this and that and I asked the girl what her name was, and in a cheeky defiant manner she looked up at me and said 'Kay!'

Her parents looked puzzled and astonished.

'What?' questioned her father.

'Where did that come from?' asked her mother.

'I've been playing with Kay!' announced the little girl.

At this point I wondered whether or not I should say something, but decided just to pretend I was as bewildered as her parents were and quickly changed the subject.

The little girl had obviously forgotten the subject and was soon going through the menu with her mum pointing out what she wanted for breakfast.

The incident wasn't mentioned again. I'm sure the parents haven't given it a second thought, but we have often thought about it and wondered if in fact she had communicated in some way with Kay.

We met up with Gordon and Gaynor again and arranged a time when the psychic artist could pay us a visit.

One of the most amazing experiences either of us have ever had was the day she came to visit us.

Christine arrived all in a flutter having struggled to find the car park (not the first time that has happened!), and thought she'd lost her handbag! She turned the car inside out before finding it wedged under the front passenger's seat.

We brought her in, put the kettle on and were in the process of making her a cup of tea when she suddenly came to a complete standstill.

'I'll have the tea later because I have Kay with me and she's nagging me to get on with the drawing; she's telling me to make it a good one so no pressure on me is there!'

With that, the lady sat down, took out a sketch pad and three pencils of differing thicknesses and took a deep breath.

Her hand began to move at a lightning speed all over the sheet of paper making lines and marks which seemed completely chaotic and random. This did not surprise us at all as she wasn't even looking at what she was doing but staring at the far corner of the ceiling.

At times, her hand would move at a high speed, then it would slow down and she would seem to spend ages focussing on just one point. We later came to realise that at his point she was concentrating on the eyes.

Eventually, she came to a standstill and put down the sketchpad, looking quite exhausted.

'I'll have that cup of tea now if you don't mind, and here's a drawing of Kay.'

She handed over the sketch to us and we were both amazed at the similarity between her and Jo – particularly around the eyes.

Interestingly, since we were made aware of Kay's existence, and have a sketch of her (which we have in a frame on the wall of our living room), no one has experienced anything in that room again.

There you go. You will all have your interpretation on this story. Some will believe and others will question – and quite rightly so.

The interesting point is that it is only as a result of living in a guest house that Kay was brought to our attention; without the experiences of those few guests, we may have never been made aware of her existence.

Chapter 14
Out and About

After several years of putting my occupation as guest house proprietor as opposed to teacher on official forms, I began to adapt to life running my own business.

The protestant work ethic that had crippled me with guilt during the early years slowly dissipated, and eventually I could enjoy going out for a walk or drink on a Monday without constantly looking over my shoulder to see who was watching me.

When I first mooted the idea of a guesthouse, the property I had in mind was an old cottage in the Yorkshire Dales. Perhaps ones full of character with beams, flagstone floors and a dog lying on the rug in front of the kitchen fire.

This was all well and good, but Jo is allergic to dogs and while these type of places do extremely well in the summer, business must die down completely in the winter.

Harrogate does not have a season as such. People come here for all sorts of reasons. Four of the country's leading wedding venues are on our doorstep, there are three theatres, spa facilities, numerous restaurants and pubs as well as the International Conference Centre.

Throughout the year, people come to Harrogate from all four corners of the globe to attend conferences hosted by the International Conference Centre. We've hosted teachers, nurses, GPs, vets, green keepers, human resource managers, weights and measure officials, and one year the Liberal Democrats when they were starting to believe they were serious opposition to the other two main parties.

Other notable events have been the numerous barber shop singers where competitors from across the country compete to win the prestigious choir of the year. Members of the White

Rosettes, a ladies barbershop group from Yorkshire have stayed with us as well as The Great Western, a men's group from the West Country.

The year the Great Western stayed with us, they won the competition and were crowned champions. I will never forget the morning they checked out. Perhaps there might have been some bleary eyes after the celebrations the previous night, but before they all departed, they congregated in our hallway and the staircase and gave us a private rendition of their award winning song.

It's magical times like this when you realise that running a guest house can be a wonderful way to make a living.

But it isn't always as glamorous or exciting as I'm sure you have gathered by now. As I sit here writing this, Jo is reminding me that there's a new door handle to replace in one of the rooms. I should have done it a long time ago, but it's one of those jobs that always seem to get pushed to the bottom of the list for one reason or other. I have no excuse. Mr Knight pointed that out to me on his first visit several years ago, and although we have done so much since then, replacing that handle has grown into some sort of monumental task that would even challenge Hercules himself.

'I promise I'll do it after I've hung this plaque,' I replied.

The last time our daughter came to visit, she brought a gift from her boyfriend's father. It was a wooden plaque with the coat of arms of the police force in Seville. He had been head of the railway police in Seville and perhaps thought people would find it an interesting talking point in our guest house. It is quite heavy, and our daughter only came over with hand luggage and even she was unsure how we would react when she presented it to us! I suppose it will be a talking point and possibly could act as a warning to any would be unruly guests.

The other curio is a life size minstrel we inherited from the previous owner. It continues to be a point of discussion though I am surprised not more people have taken offense to it. It stands as a constant reminder of times when racial equality did not exist. The majority of guests, all on a crusade to oppose political correctness pointed out that it is an integral part of our history and reflected social attitudes then as opposed to now. When we first took over the running of the guesthouse, I pointed to the minstrel and asked the then proprietor if she would be taking it with her.

'Oh no, dear,' she replied, 'Sambo stays.'

Well, if he has to say he's certainly not going to be called that, I thought.

We had one review which referred to an "iffy" statue in the hall, but other than that, there was only one customer who took real offence to it. A black comedienne from London had a real go at me as she as left one morning, pointing out that the statue was an insult to her ethnicity.

(I'd seen her on stage the previous evening, and I can assure readers that her act was simply an insult to everyone!)

Harrogate has been our home for nearly twenty years and our local knowledge of the area has helped many guests to get more out of their stay here.

I remember one couple who came to stay with us. It had been their third visit to Harrogate. Both previous visits had been at a large hotel directly opposite us, and though there had been nothing wrong with the hotel, they just thought that they would have a change.

At breakfast I suggested that because it was such a lovely day, a walk in the Valley Gardens would be ideal.

'Where?' they queried.

I pointed out on a town plan where the gardens were and I was amazed that they had been here twice and had never heard of them.

Large hotels are often staffed with people who have no local knowledge. The girl on reception at the hotel probably had never heard of the gardens herself. Perhaps she didn't even live in Harrogate herself.

Needless to say, a visit to Harrogate is not complete with a walk around the gardens. It is quite a unique place. It has more mineral springs than anywhere else in the world and they all have a completely different chemical composition. I would be hard pressed to think of anywhere with such a tranquil atmosphere. An evening walk in the gardens followed by a pint in The Old Bell Tavern is one of our favourite ways to spend an evening.

Harrogate rose to prominence after the Industrial Revolution. The invention of the steam engine and subsequent growth of the railways opened up parts of the country previously undiscovered. The mineral waters became a unique attraction and wealthy industrialists found it the ideal place to holiday, take the waters and even eventually retire to.

People still come to enjoy the Turkish Baths though they are limited to only smelling the waters from the sulphur well. There is a warning from Harrogate Borough Council pointing out that the water is not fit for drinking or consuming. Even something as sacred as this is not immune from modern day health and safety warnings!

We have enjoyed sharing the surrounding area with guests sending, them on day trips to local attractions such as Bolton Abbey, Brimham Rocks and Fountains Abbey.

Brimham Rocks were sculpted by 320 million years of ice, wind, the movement of entire continents and have subsequently taken on weird and wonderful shapes. With a little imagination, you can see familiar creatures. Visitors are encouraged to spot the dancing bear, the gorilla, the eagle and the turtle, whilst the more nimble can crawl through the Smartie tube and balance on the Rocking Stones.

I have a favourite route which I frequently share with guests who want a drive through the Dales. It has become our favourite drive and is so varied including old churches, ruined abbeys, waterfalls, cheese factories, while throwing in some amazing scenery as well.

Mike's Tour

This is our favourite Dales drive, taking in some spectacular scenery and with some interesting places to stop en-route for photographs, refreshments and meals.

Head into town to the main crossroads by The International Exhibition Centre and turn right on to the A61 road to Ripon.

At the first roundabout, turn left onto the A59 road to Skipton.

Continue on this road for half an hour or so until you reach a small roundabout – turn right for the first stop – Bolton Abbey.

There is a private car park, but worth a stop for the scenery. It is without doubt one of the most peaceful and serene places ever. Situated on the banks of the river Wharfe, the abbey was a subject of the artist Turner. The famous English cricketer, Freddy Truman is buried in the grounds of the Abbey.

From Bolton Abbey, the visitor should continue on the B6160 through the villages of Birstall, Kilnsey, Kettlewell and Buckden. This road is the route of the famous Tour de France which came to Yorkshire in 2014. In Buckden, the B6160 continues to near Aysgarth falls, but I recommend the visitor takes a left hand fork onto a small road signposted Hubberholme.

At Hubberholme, there is an amazing church from the 12th century which is worth a visit. The village was a favourite place of the writer and playwright J.B. Priestley, who described it as the 'smallest, pleasantest place in the world'. His ashes are scattered somewhere in the vicinity of the church. It has an original rood screen worth looking at – significant as most were destroyed during the reign of Elizabeth I.

Follow this small road along one of the most delightful of all the Dales, Langstrothdale. I defy anyone who stops by the river Wharfe, running parallel to this road, not to feel as though they have been transported back in time; and the area is an absolute rest cure to the stress of modern day living.

Eventually the road brings the visitor into the busy market town of Hawes with its shops, cafés and tea rooms. However, the place to stop is the Wensleydale Creamery – if only to taste the cheeses made there.

From Hawes, you can make a short detour to visit Hardraw Force. Turn left onto the A684 and you will eventually see the sign to the waterfall. Hardraw Force is England's highest unbroken waterfall and is set within the grounds of the Green Dragon Inn. The location was used in the film Robin Hood: Prince of Thieves, and those familiar with the film will recall the bit where Maid Marian catches Robin Hood (Kevin Costner) bathing under the waterfall.

Heading back to Hawes, follow the A684 through to another famous series of waterfall, the Aysgarth Falls. You have the opportunity of retracing your steps back to Kettlewell or continuing through to Masham and Ripon.

In Masham, you can visit the Theakston and Black Sheep breweries, and therefore also follow the route of Mr Mycock! The Black Sheep brewery has a great visitor's centre and an excellent restaurant.

Ripon is famous for its cathedral. The Lewis Carroll connections are worth pointing out. In the misericord, you can see many carvings which were the basis for some of the characters in *Alice in Wonderland*, including a Gryphon chasing a white rabbit down a hole!

Guests loved the route and were always enthusiastic about the things they saw and experienced. The only drawback for us is they invariably handed over a gag of cheese asking us to keep it in our fridge until they checked out. Now anyone who has tasted Wenslydale cheese will know how hard – impossible in fact – it is to resist, but every time the fridge door was open that is what I had to do.

One couple left without taking their cheese with them, but the excitement was premature when a car pulled into the car park thirty minutes later. Yes, the couple had returned to pick up their cheese (Thankfully I had not started to attack it!).

Another thing worth pointing out is that as a guest house proprietor you will end up with an amazing collection of phone and tablet chargers as this is by far the one object frequently left behind (unfortunately, the cheese was only left behind then once!).

In the early days, we would post on the charger to guests and ask them for whatever the postage cost was. Sometimes they paid, but quite often they didn't. Now we have adopted a policy of getting guests to send a stamped addressed envelope for us to post the items in.

One lady recently left an electric toothbrush. Of course she wanted us to post it on and was ready to put a cheque in the post prior to us sending it on. We informed her that it wasn't the cost that was the issue, but the inordinate amount of time it took walking and queuing in the post office: on a busy day it could take up to an hour.

The lady of course understood and we waited for the envelope to arrive, but of course it never did. It was probably cheaper to go out and buy a new one; and speaking of buying things, I really must go and get a new door handle for Room 1.

Chapter 15
Criminals and Other
Notorious Guests!

Over the ten years we have been at Holland House, we have looked after thousands and thousands of delightful guests, a handful of downright obnoxious ones and three criminals!

The criminals were all different. Only one attempted to steal from us – but thankfully didn't get away with it! Perhaps it is even unfair to label this one as a criminal and, to be honest, even the other two were more hapless fools than criminals.

The one thing they all do have in common is that they provided us with some of the most amusing, incredible tales since we took over.

One guest, many of you will have heard of and therefore know the criminal activity he is most notoriously associated with.

We received a three night booking for a twin room. The customer informed us that they would be arriving late and asked if they could have an early breakfast as they were exhibiting at a Christmas gift fair. I had gone to bed early as I knew I had to be up quite early the following morning, so Jo waited up until the customers in question arrived and escorted them to their room. When she eventually came down to bed I woke up to hear her giggling to herself. She told me that Room 7 had arrived and that she was certain it was the cheating major who had achieved notoriety on the BBC quiz programme *Who Wants to Be a Millionaire*. The programme makers' suspicions were aroused when recordings of his successful million pound win were played back, only to find that someone in the audience was coughing whenever a correct answer was read out.

The following morning, I checked and the names matched; of course when you put his name into any search engine his face (invariably alongside Chris Tarrant's!) appears for all to see.

He came down for breakfast and I pretended not to know who he was, but I instantly recognised him! Now I had to treat him just like any other guest (I already had a bit of practice at that with the Hotel Inspector). I'd brought them both coffee and was taking the order for breakfast when a large group of workers wanted to check out.

Jo went to sort out their bill and get the card machine. She was frustrated because they all wanted to pay separately. While she was processing all the payments, one of the workers peered into the dining room and in a loud voice, ordered his colleagues to look at who was sitting there in the corner eating breakfast!

With that, the four workers suddenly developed a variety of coughing ailments. One was showing signs of advanced tuberculosis, one had just swallowed something down the wrong way and the other two had a subtle tickling cough, interspersed with bouts of uncontrolled laughter.

Poor Jo did her best to remain calm, and at one point glared at the man with the loudest cough with a look that suggested a painful death would be imminent if he did not stop acting in such a childish irresponsible manner. But the truth was she didn't know where to look!

Despite everyone in the dining room turning round to see what the commotion was all about, our notorious guest continued to eat his breakfast ignoring the four spontaneous coughing bouts. Perhaps his wife had given him a weary look – I daren't look that way at all! No doubt it's something they would have experienced before, and no doubt will continue to experience – especially once the film comes out!

Another "criminal" to stay with us was also technically not a criminal, but even now, almost a year on since he stayed with us, I still find the story quite amazing.

Last year was by far the most challenging year we've had since taking over the running of the guest house. Jo was rushed into hospital with a suspected heart attack which turned out to be pancreatitis. The hospital staff were amazing, and soon had her symptoms under control and heading towards recovery – though significant life style changes would have to be made.

All this happened during one of the busiest periods of the year. I was preparing and cooking breakfasts for 14 people as well as servicing the rooms, doing the shopping, waiting to check in guests and of course visit my wife in hospital.

I contacted a supply staff agency who promised they'd send along someone to help short term, but this never materialised. Our daughter, who lived in Spain, took the next available flight home and came over to help out and to be with her mum for a week or so.

It was during this time when this most unsavoury guest stayed with us.

The man booked to stay five nights in a double room and informed us that he would be arriving at around 4pm, so there was plenty of time to do all the chores and visit Jo. Just as I was arriving in the hospital car park, I received a telephone call from a guest to say that he had arrived and was waiting outside the house but no one was answering the door. I immediately drove out of the car park and back to the guest house where I found this hapless visitor and his Goth-like girlfriend squatting on the steps waiting to be rescued.

Having checked in the one and only set of guests arriving that day, I returned to the hospital car park, knowing that I could now give all my attention to my wife. However, once again, just as I was about to put on the hand break the phone went again. It was the same number that rang last time.

This time he rang to say that there'd been an accident and somehow he had knocked the TV off the wall and the screen was completely smashed. The TV was mounted on the wall above the fireplace, so how on earth he had managed to knock into it mystified me.

I explained to him where I was and what I was doing and that I would be back later on that day – hopefully with a new TV.

After spending a couple of hours with Jo, I went straight to a nearby superstore, purchased a large screen TV and drove immediately back to replace it.

Now those of you who have had to replace a TV will know just how awkward a task it can be, but imagine having to do it with two Goths sitting in the room and commenting on every move you made. Luckily, the TV could hang on the original bracket, so there was no need for drills and all that nasty, noisy messy stuff.

The guest was grateful and pointed out that they were here on a limited budget, so would not be going out a lot in the evening. He asked if it were OK to bring back takeaways to the room. This is something we tried to discourage at first, but after a while acquiesced – thinking as long as the guests didn't make a mess (and they rarely did) we couldn't see anything wrong with it. In fact, the only negative thing for us was the smell in the room the following morning (especially if it had been a curry) and the regular trips to the local tip to get rid of the cartons (along with the numerous wine bottles and corporate printing left after many of the conferences held here).

There was something odd about the guests. I couldn't quite put my finger on it. They certainly could eat for England and made the most of breakfasts, devouring a Full English and then attacking the cereal and fruit as well as several rounds of toast.

Every morning they asked me how my wife was and even struck up conversations with some of the other guests staying. One lady, after he had gone, told me that she thought he seemed such a decent chap!

On the morning he checked out he asked if he could have a word with me. He explained that he had not brought the right debit card with him so he would struggle to pay his bill, but that he had some cash and he'd pay that and ring me when he got back home to settle the difference.

Normally this would have set the emergency bells ringing immediately, but I was so preoccupied with other things. Jo's test were still showing worrying signs which meant she would not be discharged yet and the supply agency were still not getting anywhere closer to finding me help.

I agreed to this and to be perfectly honest, thought it was the least of my worries today.

The next time I saw the guest was to see the back of his head just disappearing round the corner after he and his girlfriend had sneaked out. So much for the cash!

I had his telephone number and card details he'd used to book the room. The card was immediately declined and no one ever answered the phone. For a week or so I phoned every evening and had a go at taking payment every day for the rest of the week – all to no avail.

Now I will be quite honest and say this did get to me – more perhaps than it really should have done. It wasn't the money (or rather lack of it) that annoyed me, but that simply somebody could have behaved as such and administer such a coup de grace when I was at such a low and vulnerable point.

It was only when I mentioned this to my daughter that she came up with an ingenious idea! She asked me what his name was and with the wave of a magic wand, hey presto, there he was as large as life together with his girlfriend on Facebook!

With her help, I copied the photo, pasted it and briefly explained who he was and what he'd done.

I was about to share when my daughter stopped me.

'No dad! This'll go to just your friends. If you choose this option, then everyone on Facebook gets it!'

I could not believe this!

Everyone, everywhere in the world would be able to see his picture and read what he had done.

The button was pressed and we sat back and waited for the World Wide Web to weave its magic!

It didn't take long before comments of support and sympathy from close friends appeared. Then, people unknown to us responded with comments like 'What a twat' and 'Let's hope you track the cheating git down' as well as numerous other comments too vulgar to mention here!

Miraculously, a colleague of his responded, pointing out where he worked and that everyone knew him as a cheat and defrauder and that he was even suspected of walking off with the contents of a collection jar set up to support a local good cause.

This was proving to be very interesting and I was looking forward to receiving more information about this petty criminal when, out of the blue, the phone went.

Guess who it was?

'Mike, what's happening on Facebook?'

I explained exactly what was happening on Facebook!

'But you knew I would pay you; you had my card details. Surely you didn't think I would try to do a runner and not pay – especially after you'd looked after us so well and your wife was ill in hospital. How is she by the way?'

With that, he gave me the account details to take payment (the same details I'd had and been using all week!), and miraculously the payment went through.

I thanked him, apologised (yes, I know!) pointing out there must have been a misunderstanding and promised I would remove the post immediately.

It had been a difficult week. I wasn't even in the mood for celebrating the fact that I had finally got my money. For me it was always a matter of principal, and though I was grateful to get the payment, the fact that it had restored my belief in humanity and convinced me more people were agents of good as opposed to evil was far more important.

The third "criminal" who came to stay with us was a criminal! Jo's accurate description of him together with a positive identification at a parade confirmed this. Even so, criminal is a rather harsh term and once again, when I think of him and recall his antics – which I often do – I only smile.

He came to us during a very busy conference week. We happened to have just one single room available for the one night. A well-presented young man, he knocked on the door and informed my wife that he was looking for a single room for one night. Excellent!

Many proprietors are often reluctant to accept people who knock on the door – particularly at night (which is quite understandable), but my wife thought that the young lad looked very presentable and was well spoken. She assumed he was here on business of some sort, though when she quizzed him about his work, he deflected the questions and appeared reluctant to engage in even the most trivial of conversations. She told him the room was £40 and he accepted it immediately and produced 40 pound coins from his pocket to pay for it. Perhaps he'd had a bit of luck on the one armed bandits!

Apart from the suspicious payment, we had no further reason to be concerned until later that evening, when he was seen "snooping" around the hall and dining room, opening drawers and searching through the contents of display cabinets. and cupboards. When my wife approached him, he told her that he was looking for the number of a taxi. By then, she had his card marked.

He said he wanted to have breakfast at 9 o'clock, which is normally the latest we would serve it. However, at ten past nine he still hadn't appeared, and so my wife popped upstairs to knock on his room door: perhaps he had already left? After a couple of knocks, the door gingerly opened and the young man, completely dressed, poked his head round the door and informed her that he'd be coming downstairs immediately. She noticed that the bed hadn't been slept in at all.

Once he was downstairs, my wife ran upstairs to check his room as she thought that maybe he had been smoking. When she went into the room she got a bigger shock than she originally anticipated! On the bedside table were dozens of piles of £1 coins, each pile adding up to at least thirty pounds. Shocked, she ran downstairs and asked me to have a look. As well as the money, I noticed a large "piggy bank" standing in the corner of the room. Other than that, the room was untidy, but nothing seemed out of place or damaged.

Having already paid, the man didn't hang around and checked out fairly quickly.

My main concern was getting the room ready for our next guest whilst my wife was still wrestling with her conscience and had a hunch that all was not in order. When she first suggested that she wanted to go to the police station I thought she was being just a bit paranoid. I insisted that she make some sort of statement first – get her thoughts together before traipsing off to the cop shop. Our guest had left a lot of "stuff" in his room so we bundled it all into a dustbin bag to be taken off to the police station. Among the contents were a couple of empty wallets, some credit cards (with a different name on) and of course the piggy bank. The money had obviously gone.

I made the bed and started to clean the sink and toilet. I noticed a strange white sticky substance in the sink and assumed our guest had a thing about cleaning his teeth! It took a few goes with Vim to get everything gleaming white again. Then to my shock and horror, I saw a "make your own vagina pack to fit your own penis"!

Oh my god! That must have been stuff in the sink. I rinsed my hands immediately and shuddered to think what had been going on in that room.

The credit cards and an AA road card all had the same name on: Mr R. Huth.

With this, Jo grabbed the piggy bank and the cards and shot across to the local police station. She said it was highly ironic in that as soon as she walked into the station, a police woman behind the desk talking to someone on the telephone looked up with incredulity and said: 'The piggy bank has just walked into the police station, Mrs Huth!'

Evidently, our guest had broken into Mr Huth's home. For those readers unfamiliar with football, Robert Huth is a famous German international footballer who at the time lived in Harrogate. Our guest stole the keys to his Porsche, his wallet and of course the piggy bank. He drove 500 metres up the road before crashing the car and then walked the rest of the way, checking into Holland House and paying for the room with some of the coins.

Jo insisted he complete a registration form, which the lad did using his REAL address!

She spent nearly all day at the police station while I finished off the breakfast room and cleaned all the guest rooms (including the dodgy sink!) and didn't finish until mid-afternoon. By the time Jo arrived back, I was exhausted.

She recalled the story and I was quite excited at the prospect of Robert Huth himself paying us a visit to thank us (well, Jo actually) and who knows, handing over a couple of tickets for his next home game. (At the time, Robert Huth played for Middlesbrough I think).

Needless to say, the visit never did materialise, but at least we can all sleep in our beds safely at night knowing that Jo did her bit to ensure this country is a safer place to live in.

Chapter 16
No Regrets

So here we are, December 21st (the shortest day of the year), nearly ten years on since taking over at Holland House and the last chapter of the book. Perhaps it's a little pretentious calling them chapters? Diary logs might be more accurate – or even better, Mike's reminiscings? (Jo would say ramblings).

It's only as I sit here at the computer after repairing a shower in Room 1 and trying to fix a broken bed-side lamp in Room 5, that I can think back to when I first had the idea of running a guest house. Has it been a lot different than I envisaged? Emphatically, yes!

The physical nature of the work has been more demanding than I envisaged, but after a life of sitting at a desk, break time snacks and stodgy school meals, that is not a bad thing. It was also a semi-retirement plan though it's really turned out to be more like a full-time job – and at times the number of hours worked per week are way in excess of anything experienced in the teaching profession. However, the main difference being it doesn't seem like a real full time job; a full time job for me consisted of wearing a suit and tie and coming home with a headache!

How long can we continue running the guest house? The lady we bought the business from was well into her seventies when she finally retired, although she did employ a couple of people to do the donkey work.

To many people this would be a nightmare. Having to cook breakfasts, clear tables, clean rooms and make beds when they in their sixties. Surely people should be taking it easy at this time of life? Playing golf or bowls, doing crossword puzzles and going for holidays a few times of the year should be on the menu as opposed to dashes to the Cash and Carry or waiting up to meet guests arriving late in the evening.

People have different expectations and ideas about what retirement should be like. From my own perspective, I can only speak with reference to the numerous retired people who have stayed with us over the years.

The one thing the majority of retired people say is that they don't know how they found time to work! This suggests that these people are the active ones whose lives are filled with interesting and purposeful activities.

Of course we have the dull grey ones staying with us as well. The ones who stare at each other across the breakfast table with little or no verbal exchanges other to say thank you when their breakfasts were brought and the empty plates cleared away.

"Keep active!" was one bit of advice retired people regularly passed on by people well into their retirement. It is the secret to longevity and good health. I remember one chap working well into his '70s and running up the stairs like a spring chicken; 'It's all in here,' he told me, pointing to his head.

Certainly running up and down several flights of stairs daily helped keep us both in good health, and though Jo had a bit of a health scare a year ago. this is something we can continue to do (perhaps with a bit of additional help now and then?) for a few more years to come.

Was it the financial panacea I thought it was? Well on that one Jo was the definite winner. Money came in, but it flew out twice as quickly; I suspect isn't that everyone's experience of finances in modern day life. Certainly when we took over we'd spend a bit of money here and there on some advertising as we were totally dependent on customers ringing or emailing to book a room. Now of course, the big boys have muscled onto the scene. Companies such as Booking.com, Expedia, Late Rooms etc. all charge between 15 and 17% commission on all bookings. Certainly after the mortgage repayment, it was our largest one item of expense, but they were necessary evils and neither proprietors nor customers could live without them anymore.

Take the last Yorkshire show for example (in fact, nearly every Yorkshire show for that matter!). We blocked off the rooms online so preference is given to people phoning us directly. By doing this, we can hopefully enjoy a few days of bookings without commission to pay. Here in Harrogate it's one of the times in the year when accommodation is in very high demand. For the past several years we have literally got to a few weeks before the start of the show in early July, and still many of the rooms would not have been sold. Reluctantly we opened our rooms online (i.e. made them available on the booking sites), and usually within 24 hours all the rooms will have been sold. Maybe I should be brave enough and resist the temptation to sell early, because I can guarantee that several days before the show is due to begin, some hapless disorganised trader will be desperately ringing around, wanting several rooms for several days and we have to disappoint them – and ourselves in the process!

Without a doubt, the most important and satisfying thing for us is the people we meet. Of course you'll always get your Dr Ed Johns, your sex mad licentious creep in a grey mac, Peter and Mary (I can still smell them now) and the pretentious wine merchants from SW11, but even these people have played their small bit in putting colour and joie de vivre into our lives in one way or another. There have been hundreds and thousands of delightful and interesting people who have stayed here over the years with us and allowed us to share their lives in turn. We have had so many different people from different corners of the globe and I have enjoyed sharing this corner of North Yorkshire with them and helping them to get the most out of their stay here; this has been by far the most enriching and rewarding part of the experience.

Already, we have four Christmas cards from guests who have either stayed with us the once or who visit regularly, and here the division between customer and friend is blurred. Many people prefer anonymity when staying in guest houses – that is perfectly understandable. However, for varying reasons, these people crossed that boundary and are more than just names in the guest book.

We had a card from Professor Mike Hart and his lovely wife, Meg. They originally came to stay with us shortly after we had opened. Mike was a professor of Business Information and a visiting professor at La Coruña, in Northern Spain. Our joint interest in all things Hispanic got us off to a good start and because Meg has slight mobility issues we always say just knock

153

on the back door and come through the tradesman's entrance. That of course leads to a short delay before checking in to have a cuppa and catch up on each other's news. Since then the cuppa has evolved into a glass of wine or beer!

Mike has some hilarious stories and keeps both Jo and myself (along with other guests who happen to be in the dining room at the same time) amused with his tales. He always asks me if I've got any tales to recall, and if Professor Hart ever reads this, he'll probably be most disappointed as he will almost certainly have heard all the stories.

'I tell everyone the one about the chap you thought was a writer!' he'd often say to me, and I remember him nearly choking on his coffee when we recalled the *Who Wants to Be a Millionaire* cheat!

His wife, Meg, caused quite a stir on her most recent visit as well. After two successive mornings of eating Full English breakfasts, she decided she would have a couple of boiled eggs. We often serve boiled eggs with soldiers – no one is ever too old to have a few soldiers to dip into their eggs.

It was just unfortunate that the dining room was not only full, but also quiet when I cleared Meg's empty plate as she blurted out how she had really enjoyed having all those soldiers!

It was impossible to ignore the tittering coming from nearby tables, and Mike thought this innocent comment hilarious and even repeated what she'd said to other guests once he finally gained his composure.

'Put that down in your book, Mike,' Professor Hart cried out in earshot of everyone in the dining room.

Sorry, Meg!

Professor Hart and I share the same politics – liberal and pro-European. It's good to be able to share points of view because on the whole, I have to remain impartial when customers are talking politics. I find ways of sympathising with their views – even far right ones. Running a business of any sort involves respecting everyone regardless of their political or religious views.

Every year, we also receive a Christmas card from Michael and Sandra Saringhausen from Bremen Osterholz. They stayed the same week as Peter and Mary. This year their card folded into a lantern and when a candle is placed in the middle, all the half-timbered medieval buildings light up to produce a cosy warm winter scene. It also reminds us of the number of candles we used with our oil burners that week too!

However, some of the cards brought sad news too. In the early years of running the guest house, we enjoyed a regular yearly visit from two delightful ladies from County Durham, Alice and Margaret. All in all they had stayed with us for five or six years and their visit was always one we looked forward to.

They were warm and extremely friendly, and once we got to know them a little better, our respect grew – particularly for Alice. Alice and her husband look after two disabled sons and devote their entire life caring for them. Their few days in Harrogate was a respite for Alice; a chance for her to get away and have a giggle with Margaret. We learnt that Alice and her husband ran a pub together, but things got very difficult in the early 1990s. Black Wednesday, or Wednesday 16 September 1992, was the day when the British Conservative government was forced to withdraw the pound sterling from the European Exchange Rate Mechanism (ERM). Interest rates soared and at one point reached 15 to 16%. This resulted in many home owners and businesses unable to pay back their mortgages, and during this time many people, including Alice and her husband, not only lost their business but their home as well.

However, despite experiencing such hardship, Alice never allowed this to spoil her zest for life and her enduring sense of fun. She looked after Margaret, who had been single all her life and was in many ways naïve and less worldly than Alice – though they could both giggle for England and looked forward to a tipple in the evening.

This last visit had been more stressful for Alice and she pointed out to us that she could see signs of Margaret deteriorating. She had become more forgetful and somehow didn't seem as "with it" as she had been in previous years. She had never been as "full on" as Alice was but Margaret too could have her moments. It seemed that these moments were growing fewer and Alice had to remind her constantly where they were going to visit during the day or going to eat during the evening, and she even had to take control of her spending money. Alice made sure Margaret paid her half of the room before they left fearing that she'd blow it all on needless souvenirs.

The news in the Christmas card was sad. Margaret had deteriorated rapidly shortly after returning to Durham and Alice thought that it would not be long before she would need 24/7 care and supervision. She thanked us for the wonderful memories we had given them, but she was sorry to say that this year would be their last visit as she could no longer be responsible for her.

Sad news but something everyone everywhere has to deal with at some point in their lives – especially with older relatives.

One of the hardest things about running a business, especially a business of this nature, is the extent to which you do become involved in peoples' lives.

Rightly or wrongly, we were first and foremost peoples' people and so our raison d'être was meeting people and enjoying conversations on a wide variety of topics however fleeting or brief. It is an art, rather than a science, knowing when someone wants to engage in conversation or would rather keep themselves to themselves. We soon learnt to respect the anonymity some folk wished to keep whenever they went away for a few days; in the early days Jo would often come to the dining room to find me in deep conversation with guests and whispered that I might want to leave them to get on with their breakfasts in peace!

Some guests however, were all too eager to join in the conversations. I especially enjoyed talking to ex-teachers and sometimes Jo would come along to the dining room an hour after breakfast had finished to find us banging fists on tables (metaphorically of course!) and moaning about the way things are going in education.

Not every teacher had the luxury of being retired and I remember one particular weekend when two couples had booked a Saturday night out together and we set a table of four for the following morning at breakfast. It's often easy to see who has had a good night out and who hasn't! (I remember one German guy after a very heavy night sitting at the table and falling asleep with his face in the left over baked beans on his plate – but that's another story!).

It wasn't difficult to see that that three of the foursome were having a splendid time while one chap was totally uncommunicative. In fact, the only thing he said at breakfast time was to look up and order a Full English. I was about to ask him if he would prefer white or wholemeal toast but guessed that even this would be one step too far.

Obviously, I was concerned that his mood might have something to do with us. Had we in any way, knowingly or unknowingly, contributed to his severe depression, though the fact that his wife and the other couple were giggling away suggested this was not the case.

I eventually managed to whisper to his wife and asked if everything was OK or was there anything we could do as the guest was obviously unhappy with something when she explained that her husband was a deputy head and Ofsted were inspecting his school the next day. As soon as they got home, he would go straight to school, she informed me.

My sympathy. Been there and got the T shirt!

The fourth Christmas card we received from guests who had stayed with us was by far the most emotional. It had not been posted and arrived on a Sunday afternoon – pushed through the letter box by hand.

It was a very simple card and inside was the inscription:

'To Mr and Mrs Ganley, thank you for the kindness you showed to us last year,' and signed Mr and Mrs Wright.

Goodness me, was it had been a whole year since they stayed with us!

They, or to be exact, he, arrived on his own on a Wednesday evening. It was about 7:30 and of course being December, was quite dark and very cold. Mr Wright asked how much a double room for the night would be and when I told him, he looked thoughtful and asked whether or not the room would be cheaper if they didn't have breakfast. I sensed something wasn't right, but explained that breakfasts were £5 each and so the room would be £10 cheaper than the price quoted.

He said he'd collect his wife who was sat in the car outside.

When they eventually appeared in the main hall, I went to give them a hand carrying their suitcases up to the room. I was busy going through the usual blurb I had spouted out thousands of time: en-suite, Wi-Fi code, tea and coffee making facilities when the lady burst into tears.

Her husband looked up and explained that his wife was a little emotional as they had been made homeless that week. He told me that they had slept in the car for three nights and his wife had spent the days in the local library when he went to work. I got a shock when he said this as we invariably associate all homeless people as being unemployed; lazing around all day doing nothing and therefore completely responsible for the mess they had found themselves in.

However, this was not your archetypal homeless man. For a start he was probably in his early sixties and he held down a full time job. It was a shock to me to think that this could happen to anyone in this country and there, but for the grace of God, we go. Most of us can choose to ignore things like this, and the only time we are confronted by homelessness is coming across someone sitting on a blanket in any one of our towns and cities across the country asking for small change.

I felt a surge of emotion. Above all, I felt some sort of responsibility.

The gentleman got out his wallet and I immediately told him to put it away and that I hoped they could have a warm shower, a good nights' sleep and insisted that I saw them in the breakfast room the following morning.

At this stage, I hope you, the reader, do not think that this story has been included because it's a good tear-jerker or because it will put me in some sort of "better light"; it's far too late for me to be seeking redemption of any sorts now!

I include this story simply because it happened. Had I been living in a normal house, then I wouldn't have been aware of Mr Wright or other people in a similar situation.

The couple ended up staying three nights with us, but when it came to Saturday we were fully booked up and had been for some weeks. Mr Wright explained that the council had arranged some temporary accommodation, but before he checked out he insisted on paying me.

I obviously refused to take any payment and asked if he had enough money for him and his wife to get something to eat or at least to see them through until their next pay day. He confirmed that he had and drew out £25 from his wallet. He said it will only go a small way to meet the costs, but he insisted that I take the money. Once again, I was about to refuse but saw the fierce pride in his eyes. Refusing the money would be to destroy the last vestige of pride the man had and, ashamedly, I took the twenty-five pounds from him.

The last guest checked out that morning and we were all on our own until after Christmas. I bolted the front door, locked the inner door before turning the sign around to "Sorry, we are full". This was always a very satisfying thing to do. Of course we needed the guests to help pay the mortgage and keep the wheels turning but there was something very special knowing you were on your own and more importantly, didn't have to get up in the morning to prepare breakfast!

Our son, Ben, his partner, Claudia, and our little granddaughter, Amelia, would be flying in from Berlin later on that afternoon. In the evening, our daughter, Sanne, her partner, Juan Luis, and their daughter and our granddaughter, Lena, would be arriving on the flight from Malaga. It was to be a real international time in Harrogate though fish and chips, curries and a few bottles of Old Peculier would feature high on the agenda.

Time to clean all the rooms, get the dishwasher and bag all the soiled sheets ready for collection that morning before sitting down to a well-earned cup of coffee and a first mince pie of the season.

With a bit of luck, I might even get round to putting a new door handle on in Room 1!